Praise for
MOTHER NOISE

"Raw and tender . . . *Mother Noise* feels lovingly labored over, expertly whittled and chiseled into its current frank form. . . . Here's a book not about how you rebuild yourself through writing but about how writing itself can be a kind of rebuilding, a reassembling of your past mistakes."

—*The New York Times*

"A beautiful tribute to real life . . . phenomenal."

—Tamron Hall, *Tamron Hall Show*

"Unexpectedly uplifting. . . . In her masterfully crafted memoir, House includes stories of despair and joy. Ultimately, the narrative she shared with her son also brings hope to her readers."

—*Shelf Awareness* (starred review)

"Exalting art, our families, and ourselves, House's writing is serious with room for lightness, polished without sacrificing sincerity. Memoir devotees will find it hard to put down."

—*Booklist* (starred review)

"A brutal story of heroin addiction gives way to a heartening look at motherhood in this brilliant debut from essayist House. . . . A full-throated anthem of hope, this lends light to a dark issue."

—*Publishers Weekly* (starred review)

MOTHER NOISE

❧ Cindy House ❧

**MARYSUE
RUCCI
BOOKS**

New York   London   Toronto   Sydney   New Delhi

**MARYSUE
RUCCI
BOOKS**

An Imprint of Simon & Schuster, Inc.
1230 Avenue of the Americas
New York, NY 10020

Copyright © 2022 by Cindy House

First Marysue Rucci Books trade paperback edition May 2023

MARYSUE RUCCI BOOKS and colophon are trademarks of Simon & Schuster, Inc.

For information about special discounts for bulk purchases, please contact Simon & Schuster Special Sales at 1-866-506-1949 or business@simonandschuster.com.

The Simon & Schuster Speakers Bureau can bring authors to your live event. For more information or to book an event, contact the Simon & Schuster Speakers Bureau at 1-866-248-3049 or visit our website at www.simonspeakers.com.

Interior design by Carly Loman

Manufactured in the United States of America

10 9 8 7 6 5 4 3 2 1

Library of Congress Cataloging-in-Publication Data has been applied for.

ISBN 978-1-9821-6875-9
ISBN 978-1-9821-6877-3 (pbk)
ISBN 978-1-9821-6880-3 (ebook)

The events described in these stories are real. Some characters are composites and some have been given fictitious names and identifying characteristics in order to protect their anonymity.

Earlier versions of some stories appeared in the following publications: "After the Telling" in *The Rumpus*; "Turnpike" in *Lily Poetry Review*; "Comfort in Stories" in *Literary Mama*; "The Salton Sea" in *Driftwood Press*; "Vodka Vodka Vodka" in *Wigleaf*; and "Rated M for Mature" on the website *On the Seawall*.

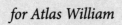

for Atlas William

CONTENTS

MOTHER NOISE

After the Telling

In February 2017, standing in an elementary school caf- eteria under a ceiling full of tissue paper–and-cellophane jellyfish, I decided I had to tell my nine-year-old son, Atlas, that I had once been a heroin addict.

I watched the crowd of kids do the Dab in unison to the DJ's loud dance music. They all looked so much older on the dance floor, so different from the huddle of children squatting over a pile of Legos that they had been just last year.

My friend watched her son bend and twist next to mine. She told me about her impending divorce, holding her baby girl, who squealed with the music.

"I think he's struggling," she said, watching her son. She looked gaunt and anxious. I wondered how much weight she'd lost. She shifted the baby to her other hip. "I just want my kids to be okay in spite of our stupid adult crap."

On the dance floor, I watched my boy trying to catch on to the moves his friends were doing. All the kids' arms went up in the air and he followed, a beat behind.

If I don't tell him soon, it could become a lie by omission, a distance between us, a secret that might leave him feeling like he doesn't really know me.

The girls in my son's third-grade class pummeled him with balloons, circling him and abandoning their dance steps.

It might take me months to work up to it, but I had to tell him.

ↄ

A few years before, a writer friend's kind, musical, lovely twenty-three-year-old son had died by suicide after a long struggle with addiction. Because I know my friend was an excellent, empathic, involved mother who did everything she could to save her son, I began to worry about mine. It was as if the threads of our lives suddenly knit together and now the future awaiting my son and me was terrifying.

I have barely mentioned Atlas to this friend in seven years. She has told me how thoughtless people can be. She said one friend would email her photos of her little boy with the subject line, "This will cheer you up." Sometimes seeing pictures of this other woman's seven-year-old in rain boots, on the beach, holding flowers out to the camera, sent my friend to her bed for days.

I did not tell my friend that my son's therapist would say to me, on bad days, "But your child is not her child."

I carry the possibility of disaster, the worry about what *could* happen, even as my friend gets up every day in spite of what *did* happen.

ↄ

Yesterday, I saw a very informative video of a little girl demonstrating how to break zip ties binding her wrists with just the laces in her shoes. She was tiny, maybe eight years old or so. But she freed herself easily, with very little effort.

Should I show my son this video? Will he ever have a reason to need this information?

When my boy was three, I taught him that if someone should try to take him, if anyone picked him up and started to carry him off, he should not scream the word *help* but should instead scream, "This is not my parent!" I taught him to look for a mother with children should he become lost and find himself without me in a crowd.

کر

Preparing to tell Atlas means thinking about that future conversation a lot. He'll be ten on his next birthday. I am about to try to publish a memoir that spells it out. If I don't tell, he could hear it from someone else.

My son likes to let people know that his first word was book. As a writer, I love that this was his first meaningful word. What if his first word had been *no*? And what if I was the kind of mother who would tell the story of his first word being *no* to get others to laugh at his defiant quality, some inherent naughtiness already present when he was a baby? Could this have changed who he is, how he sees himself?

There is evidence that addiction can be hereditary. When he knows my history, will he grow up and tell a new story about himself, feel an obligation to live out that which he sees as his fate? We want to protect our children from everything.

کر

I have a video about addiction being a faulty coping skill, the result of trauma or neglect being imprinted on the addict.

I read a book about how recovering parents can talk to their children about their addiction.

I see myself sitting next to Atlas, maybe on our front steps.

Here. Come sit with me. Let's share a tangerine. Let me tell you how sad I used to be and all the ways I tried to disappear and how it almost worked.

These are things my son already knows about me: In elementary school, the other kids called me Cindy Mouse because I was timid. I hyperventilated often from trying not to cry. I liked to line up hundreds of my Fisher-Price people and then spend whole afternoons moving them one at a time, inch by inch, because it helped me think. I was afraid of balls flying at me, girls whispering behind my back, my mother's temper. I could not ride a bike until I was nine. Once, at summer camp, I was thrown into the deep end of the swimming pool as a method of instruction, probably because the teenage camp counselors were sick of my anxiety. In college, when I could not stop crying, I went to a hospital for one long winter where they locked me inside to keep me safe.

What he doesn't know: I was a heroin addict on and off for seven years in my twenties and thought I'd never stop.

&

At age five, my son started having meltdowns several times a day and tantrums when he had to go to his father and stepmother's house. I told him stories about my own meltdowns as a child.

I told him about the time I lost my shit on the school bus because my mother had shoved me out the door in the pouring rain in boots I hated and did not want to wear. Before the bus even left my street, I was hyperventilating in my seat. The bus driver stopped the bus and made my older brother come to the front to sit with me, thinking that would calm me. With everyone staring, I could not get control of myself. My son listened to this story, still wiping away his own tears. The next day, as we sat at the table drawing together, he said, "Mom, what was wrong with the boots?"

꙳

It is only now that I am thinking of how to tell him about my past that I realize how much danger I was in back then.

When I was twenty-four, I broke my jaw in three places when I fell off the railing-less second floor of my loft space because I was drunk. The nurses discharged me with a little kit that held wire cutters and pliers. They told me to carry it with me at all times while my jaw was wired shut in case I got sick. I shoved it in a drawer and forgot about it.

The week I was unwired and could open my mouth again, I suddenly had this vivid image of what it might be like to vomit with your jaw wired firmly shut. For the first time, I realized that a person could die like that and it wouldn't be a nice way to go. I was so self-destructive and so rarely sober that I either didn't care if I died or I was incapable of thinking things through to their likely conclusions.

I spent years trying to kill myself. Now I want to live forever, at least long enough to see my child grow into adulthood and not need me anymore. In my opinion, I am all that my son has, his only responsible parent. He is sensitive the way I was and I feel a pressing need to arm him with my understanding and kindness until he is strong enough to handle the cruelty and meanness in this world without inflicting it on himself as a way to try to cope with it.

꙳

On the radio, I heard a report about pediatricians who are being trained to treat refugee children. They talked about a five-year-old Syrian boy who was afraid to go outside, who cowered and hid whenever he heard sirens. His father said that sirens meant bombs to the child and no amount of reassurance from his parents could convince him there were no bombs in America. They could try to feed him the information they thought he needed to alter himself for this new environment but they could not make him believe it. Did they worry that he would stay this way forever? Or were they so happy to know he was no longer in danger of dying in the rubble of a collapsed building that they did not give more than a passing thought to his now-unnecessary fear?

❧

I'm not afraid my son will love me less. I am not afraid of his judgment. I am afraid of his sorrow. I am afraid of the part of him that feels everything so intensely. He gave half of his book fair money to the only child in class who had none, even though it was against the rules to do so. How torn he must have been, my son who likes to follow rules, when faced with the sadness of one boy having nothing while everyone else bought new things.

Maybe late at night when he can't sleep, he will struggle to put me in a new costume of someone who is haunted and trying to destroy herself. The effort will alter something inside of him, some little place that used to be safe from pain but is now cracked open.

The world is inhospitable and can make us want to disappear, and knowing this could prepare him enough to save himself. But what if the information about my past works not as a warning but instead as a blueprint?

🖝

If the worst thing actually happens, then what? Is surviving trauma a constant settling and readjusting, an effort to accept that which is unacceptable? But how far can that go? Are there things we cannot adjust to? Or do we recalibrate for absolutely everything that can happen to us?

My ten-year-old had no money for the book fair, but he came home with books anyway.

My son became an addict and died far from home, but I have sweet memories.

Bombs destroyed our life but we made it to a new country so it's okay if my kindergartener lives under his bed.

🖝

At the elementary school dance, my son and I waited in line for the photo booth. I paid the five dollars, pulled back the curtain, and sat down inside with my child. A sign said there would be three shots taken with a countdown on the screen before each flash.

Three, two, one, and the shock of yellow light washing over us, exposing us, blinding us.

When I held the damp strip of photos in my hand and my kid went back to his friends on the dance floor, I stared at our faces. My son looked like the sweet boy he was at three and four and five. His face was open, his smile joyful, his eyes bright. In each shot, my expression is serious and I lean toward him with my mouth open, as if I am rushing to tell him everything he needs to know about this world. He smiles at the camera, blissfully oblivious. This will be the last time he poses with me unaware of who I was in the years before he came to me with all the wonder and joy I had no right to ever hope for. I look at us in the strip of photos, certain that we will still be able to recognize each other after the telling.

Nathan Hale
"Under
the Sea"
February 11, 2017

Slides

MY FAMILY DIDN'T HAVE PHOTO ALBUMS; WE HAD SLIDES. MY father was usually the photographer and the projectionist. I can still hear the sound of the carousel moving through our memories, shining the images on the wall in a dark room. *Ka-sheek. Ka-sheek.* Going through old boxes of slides, I find a few of the whole family and wonder who took the camera from my dad's hands and snapped the picture.

I am the only addict in my immediate family. My father was addicted to cigarettes and tried but failed to quit many times. I wouldn't say he was an addict in the way that I was, but he lost his life to smoking. He never saw me in recovery and he never met his grandchildren.

The slides are photos of his tomato plants, his golf trips in the eighties with men in monochromatic pastel colors on vast stretches of perfect green, our house after record-breaking snowstorms, the graduations and proms of me and my brother, a few vacations and day trips we took as a family, and deer hunting with male relatives in upstate New York.

This is my mother, brother, and me pretending to be locked in the stockade at Old Sturbridge Village in the late seventies on a hot summer day. All three of us look sweaty and miserable in the photo, as if we really are prisoners.

I find a slide from a trip we took to Washington, D.C., with another family when I was three. My mother likes to tell a story from this trip about how the little girl from the other family wet her pants and I wouldn't let her borrow a spare pair of mine.

There are a few slides from birthdays. I see this one and guess that I am being told to sit like a lady in my dress. Beloved toys are scattered in these photos, newly unwrapped. This brings back a flood of memories, as if my toys were my true connections back then.

Baby Alive, with her hard plastic limbs and movable mouth, boxed with a bottle and diapers and packets of baby food. The toy company, Kenner, claimed that its focus group of little girls found the toy both irresistible and disgusting. The commercial had this line: "Baby Alive needs a diaper change! She really dirties it!" I remember the smell of her slippery yellow hair. I also remember the chemical taste of her baby food. Of course I ate it.

I remember the way the colors of my Big Wheel faded into muted versions of themselves before the end of the first summer I owned it.

I had a collection of Madame Alexander dolls from other countries, but I had to play with them in secret because they were collector's items and I wasn't supposed to ruin them. I named them and created an apartment building for them on a wicker bookshelf in my room.

I loved my Fisher-Price people the best. I used them like a drug, a way of soothing the edges of my anxiety. I would line them all up and make them pass through their play town, moving them one by one, inch by inch. This tedious activity that I knew not to perform in front of others calmed me, helped me think. I would sometimes crave it when I was away from home, and I still feel a kind of peace just remembering the feel of the plastic figures in my hand.

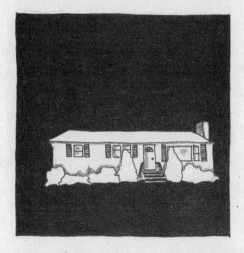

I don't know why I was so anxious. We lived in a normal house in a normal neighborhood. I had plenty of toys, neighborhood kids to play with, parents who were home with us every night.

My extended family on my mother's side lived two hours away and we saw them often.

We saw my dad's side of the family in the summer.

On the surface, things seemed fine. But something was wrong.

I look through the slides, studying my face as a child, searching for some kind of clue.

I go further back. In so many of the images, my face looks worried or sad. There's no easy answer to be found, no one clear reason.

Everyone's unhappiness filtered down to the smallest member of the family and the residue sat inside me, with nowhere else to go. It rotted for years and years.

My feelings were unacceptable, a burden and bother to others. As a child, even as a very young child, I knew that I felt things too intensely, in a way that was clearly not normal, and it angered and embarrassed people around me. I found ways to numb out early on, to interrupt emotion. I learned that it was useless to try to explain how I felt or what I needed, so I tried to take care of myself the best way I could.

I went to camp in the summer and felt terrorized. I was afraid of the water, afraid of the dark, afraid of fire. One year on a hike, someone pointed out poison sumac. I grabbed leaves of it and rubbed it all over my face and arms, thinking this might keep me home for the rest of camp. It didn't work because it probably wasn't poison sumac after all.

I think my family didn't know what to do about me.

My anxiety morphed and changed as I grew, from bitten nails to insomnia to eating issues. I tried to grow up around its parameters, drawing and writing to escape its symptoms and demands.

I find a curious graduation photo in the pile of slides. I seem to be standing away from my peers, away from the bleachers. I'm holding my diploma, so the ceremony must have ended. I don't recognize the suited men in the photo and have no idea why one of them is grabbing my arm and the other looks on with concern. My face in the photo is glued to the hand on my arm and my smile looks frozen, fearful. I look at this photo and imagine the man saying something like, "The world is going to eat you alive and everything that you are afraid of and more will happen to you." He probably said something closer to, "Hey, congratulations, good luck in the future." To my ears, back then in 1985, it was the same thing.

Damen Avenue

A LONG TIME AGO, I LIVED IN A NEIGHBORHOOD IN CHICAGO called Wicker Park. This was before addiction, before rehab, before bridges were blazed and blackened. Living there, I had to walk up Damen Avenue every day to catch the train.

Wicker Park is completely different now, but back then, under the L tracks at Damen and North and Milwaukee, the Busy Bee was still there serving breakfast to hungover twenty-somethings and neighborhood working people. The Red Dog was where we sometimes danced. Leo's Lunchroom, on Division, was the best deal in the neighborhood, and Urbis Orbis served all-day coffee refills. My asshole ex-boyfriend had a tattoo shop in the Flat Iron Building on Milwaukee and I'd have to look at his stupid neon sign whenever I went up that way.

If you're reading this and you happened to live in Chicago anywhere between the late eighties and the mid-nineties, you are probably nodding your head and picturing these places. Maybe you've eaten toast and scrambled eggs at the Busy Bee and tipped the nice Polish waitresses. Maybe Hans poured you a drink at the Red Dog. Maybe you even got a tattoo from my awful ex-boyfriend, who was a pretty good tattoo artist, from what I heard.

Not a full-blown addict yet, this was when what I was doing could be called self-medicating, mostly with alcohol, plus any drug

I stumbled upon, but nothing set on a regular schedule of doses. Nobody had said the word rehab yet; I hadn't even thought it at that time.

I lived in various apartments in that neighborhood. Across from the Rainbo Club for a while, then I moved to Noble Street and then Blackhawk and then Hoyne, where I lived with a friend, a young single mother, and her two small children. We had opposite work schedules and our lives intersected just enough to make it work. The children were beautiful and funny, and although I was only twenty-five, I was so sure I'd never have my own kids that I viewed it as my one window into what I would be missing.

Chicago is a city full of terrible memories for me. And then there is one pocket of time when I walked up Damen Avenue every day.

Springtime. Beautiful weather. Sun shining. I stroll up the street, in no rush. In an empty lot on Damen that I passed daily, on this one perfect day, someone had left a couch in the tall grass. A piece of furniture in decent shape, not torn up or filthy or wet or anything, just sitting in the lot, upright, like it had been carefully delivered.

And maybe the next day or a few days later, I walk by the same overgrown lot and someone had added a coffee table. Placed right in front of the couch as if anyone might put her feet up or set down her cup of tea.

And another day passed, or maybe a couple of days. I see a floor lamp added. An armchair. A bookshelf. A rug. A side table. A coatrack.

There was a living room arranged in the weeds, which had been stomped down a bit with all of the moving of furniture. It was like you could just sit down for a while if you needed to think things over, before you made a mistake.

I never really have anywhere to be in the memory. I never discuss it with anyone walking by and no one stops to stare but me. I just stand there, seeing the items in the empty lot.

I don't know who did it, if it was one person or a bunch of people who decided to add things. Maybe they were Raymond Carver fans and loved his story "Why Don't You Dance?" The story goes like this: a middle-aged man sets up his furniture on his front lawn to sell it when a young couple comes along, interested in the items.

I like to think that Damen Avenue setup was a community effort. I want to think of that city in just this one way, my only true Chicago. Me, standing in the sunlight, the breeze in my hair, stopped on the cracked sidewalk, long before addiction almost killed me, long before I wanted addiction to kill me, the city full of possibility and spectacle.

Maybe someone is reading this who set the rug down, brought the armchair, who arranged the end table just so. I like to imagine that, too. Someone out there somewhere whispering, *That was me, I was part of that, I remember, too.*

I've sat through movies because they were filmed in places that I knew. I have leaned forward in my seat in a dark theater, hungry for something familiar, the house, the street, the park, the skyline, the cliff by the ocean, the way the clouds are only that shade of gray *there*. I've looked for a landscape that I recognize the way I might search for the face of a loved one in a crowd.

If my years in Chicago were a filmstrip of still images, linked and rushing together, I can say that more than two decades of time passing have left me with the ability to cut out and splice together a few seconds of a purer, happier memory, separated and standing alone now. The blip on the screen where I can catch a glimpse and feel flooded with something better than regret or shame.

We Waitresses

I WENT BACK TO CHICAGO FOR THE FIRST TIME IN MORE THAN ten years because I wanted to show my son the city where I went to college and spent much of my young adulthood. We stayed in a hotel on Michigan Avenue, near the museums I thought he'd like, and far away from the neighborhoods where most of my bad memories lived. I wanted to fly in and out, like a tourist, like someone who had only good, new things to see.

But our hotel was near Ontario Street, where I'd worked in a restaurant during the worst years of my life. Let's call this restaurant Scales. It was the kind of place that catered to convention visitors, orthodontists from Dubuque and Kansas City, salesmen from Omaha and Toledo. I never thought the food was good. It was raw oysters and prime rib, overpriced lobster tails and vacuum-packed escargot. This was not farm-to-table, a menu based on local, fresh ingredients. Instead, everything served came frozen in boxes, carted off a truck parked in the back alley.

I applied for the job when I moved back to Chicago after a long stay in a psychiatric ward when I was twenty-three. Bloated from all the psychotropic drugs they had me on, I didn't fit in my clothes. I had cut my hair off right before the hospital. I felt as far from who I had once thought I was as I could ever imagine. I wanted to work at Scales because I knew I would not have to worry about memorizing the ingredients of gastronomic masterpieces or fussed-over wine lists curated by a degreed sommelier. I could just make money as the mess that I was until I shifted back toward myself, if that was even possible anymore.

The chef was not trained; he was some guy named Fabrice who hit on all of us waitresses and bullshitted the small-town clientele, those pharmaceutical executives and anesthesiologists letting loose during their yearly big-city convention. I watched his hands, when he spoke to me, the way you might watch a bee out of fear it could land on you and sting you.

The restaurant, dwarfed by the high-rise buildings around it, was a town house with two floors, a bar and casual tables at basement level and a fancier dining room above. There was a mezzanine level for the entrance where a giant window faced the sidewalk, the name Scales painted on the front, the glass showcasing a bin of crushed ice cradling crab legs, giant Indonesian shrimp, and tightly closed oyster shells.

While working there, I went back to school part-time and took an independent study with the writing teacher I'd had before the hospital. This happened to be a not-yet-famous David Sedaris before he moved to New York, when he was teaching at the School of the Art Institute of Chicago. I wrote a story based on Scales. I imagined a waitress named Bird, a total wreck of a girl, and I put her with a construction guy who was hired to rip out a wall in the upstairs dining room in the middle of the night after the restaurant closed. I don't have a copy of the story anymore, but I remember I gave the worker a gun and I named him Guy and at the end of the story, just when you think Guy is a danger to Bird, she picks up his gun and holds it straight out, posing with it, and she says to Guy,

"How do I look?" I remember David saying that Guy had "no idea who he has just armed." And I realized that Bird, who was some piece of me the way characters always are, was absolutely fucking crazy. I didn't even realize how crazy she was until I knew how David saw her. They say that when you dream, everyone in the dream is some part of you. Story characters are the same.

In the story, I wrote about rats flowing into the dining room the night Guy tears the first section of wall down. At the real Scales I never saw rats, but we suspected they might be in the walls. The building was old. Late at night, when the music was turned off and we were checking out, we heard strange noises in the drywall sometimes. The dining room and the bar looked okay in the dim lights, but the kitchen was filthy and coolers were always breaking down. It was small, dingy, and full of pipes crossing the ceiling, like the inside of a submarine. We had to move carefully around each other just to retrieve dinner salads or pick up food on the line.

We all smoked through our shifts. In the wait stations behind the dining rooms, mostly hidden from customers, we left our burning cigarettes in overflowing ashtrays so we could just return to them for another drag after opening a bottle of wine or taking an order. This was the early nineties when restaurants had smoking sections. At Scales, only four tables at the very front of the second-floor dining room were technically nonsmoking.

The staff also drank on the job. We waitresses generally held off until near the end of a shift but the three bartenders drank straight through. They were the kind of drinkers who had learned how to function in front of people, even when they remembered nothing of it the next day because they had worked through a drunk blackout. They bartended on automatic. Completely wasted and still walking up to each new guest, throwing down the white paper cocktail napkin, and saying, "What'll it be?" And they could still get the math right at closing time when they paid out the credit card tips to each server.

Of the three bartenders, Raoul was the worst. One night after I'd worked a double and had drinks with the other waitresses at the bar next door, I was walking to a convenience store in the neighborhood to pick up a pack of smokes before I got in a cab to go home. I saw a pickup truck stopped at a green light. There was no other traffic, no one behind the truck honking their horn. As I got closer, the light changed back to red and I saw that the driver had his forehead resting on the steering wheel. The light changed back to green just as I got to the truck and saw it was Raoul, passed out in the driver's seat.

His window was open and I tapped his shoulder.

"Hey, Raoul," I said.

He sat right up and said, "Have a good night, now, thanks for coming." Then he drove off through the intersection and into the night.

We waitresses weren't much healthier. There was Danielle, an actress, with a boyfriend named Spark, a lead singer in a band and a recovering alcoholic. He didn't want Danielle to drink, so she hid it. At a show one night, I watched Spark glare at her from the stage as she drunkenly moved to the music. He jumped off the stage, crashing into the two of us, and grabbed her by the upper arm, dragging her out of the bar. The crowd went crazy, thinking it was part of the act.

There was Corinne, whose boyfriend attacked her one night, long after the rest of us tried to tell her he was bad news. She said she'd left him and moved to a shelter, but then she quit and none of us heard from her again, which made us suspect that she had stayed with him even after he put her in the hospital. There was Janice, whose husband cooked cocaine they freebased together on her nights off. And Mary, my favorite, the only one of us who freely admitted to being a massive fuckup.

There was one time when a normal person was hired as a waitress. Stephanie was young, a college student who talked about tough exams she had coming up, with long shiny blond hair and expensive jewelry and shoes and what we guessed was a wealthy fiancé. She lasted a week, and in that time we would stare at her and ask her questions and compliment her on the outfits she changed into after her shifts, as if we were prisoners and she was bringing us news of the world from the outside.

Sometimes the two old Chicago guys who owned Scales ran wine contests. Whoever sold the most bottles of a particular kind of wine would be sent home with one for themselves. We never tried very hard because it was usually terrible wine anyway, bottles they were just trying to get rid of. And the winner would be called Wine Slut of the Month. Every time. As if this were still funny the seventy-third time they said it.

The owners routinely called us sluts and whores, commented on the fit of our pants, the state of our love lives, the way the male clientele, those conventioneers from out of town, treated us or talked about us. It was as if Scales advertised oysters Rockefeller with a side of slut-shaming, an appetizer of harass-your-waitress. It was as if there were fine print at the bottom of each menu announcing that it was the only restaurant in Chicago where you were encouraged to degrade your server, even paw her if you were so inclined. I could list the ways the owners harassed us, and encouraged customers to do the same, for another ten pages. I could talk about the time I broke my jaw and went back to work while my jaw was still wired shut, because I had bills to pay, and how they loved the new material my damaged face gave them, the way they could tell so many jokes about my diminished worth now that I was unable to perform blow jobs. I could talk about how vicious they were to Barbara, an older waitress with gray hair and extra pounds, someone they bullied both for being a sexual object because she was female but also for not being a very good sexual object because she was no longer young. I watched her sometimes and wondered if she was blocking it out as successfully as she appeared to be, and if so, how did she do that? How did any of us do that?

But I never asked her. We waitresses never discussed the rampant harassment, the demeaning behavior inflicted on us. We all sort of pretended it wasn't happening. At the most, we rolled our eyes and shook our heads and lit another cigarette.

I could list all of their transgressions, but why? It's not even very interesting. This is what many men do to women. We are all aware of this.

When I graduated from my MFA program in June 2017, I started sending work out. I had an easier time getting essays accepted for publication than short stories. I never wrote a sentence of nonfiction until I was working on my master's degree. When I asked David if he had any advice on whether I should look for an agent with a collection of essays rather than stories, he told me that my essays always had a narrator who was very smart and my stories seemed to have narrators who were more passive, just letting life happen to them.

He was right.

I started writing stories when I was eighteen. It was a place to put the terrible things I noticed in the world. As if I believed that I could not act, that I had no agency, but I could still write down the facts of what happened to me. Maybe I hadn't allowed my fictional characters to grow out of that silence. But I could now. Just as I would never tolerate the environment I endured at Scales in my current life, perhaps I could give my characters the same freedom from abuse. Who could Bird be now? What could she do with that life I made for her in that old story?

After a year or so, I left my job at Scales when I received a settlement for my broken jaw from the fall off the second floor of my loft. I was not a girl who should have had that lump sum put into my hands. I slipped into addiction, which was a comfortable place to be, like a tepid bath when you're too tired to sleep.

A couple of years after I'd left the job, when I was fresh out of my first rehab that wouldn't end up sticking, I got a call from a woman who worked for the Equal Employment Opportunity Commission. Some of my previous coworkers had initiated a complaint and a lawsuit against the owners of Scales for sexual harassment.

"Would you say this was a hostile work environment?" the woman asked.

"Worse than you can imagine," I said.

She asked for examples and then she asked for complaints about specific men.

I was white-knuckling my way through another day of not using in my first month of sobriety. I had time to talk. I had nothing better to do. I had questions of my own, like who spoke first and what did they say and what kind of money are we talking about here. The addict inside perked up. A previously unidentified financial resource to buy me another period of blessed self-medication.

When I wrote my story about Scales almost thirty years ago, I had a scene where a door swings open into a waitress carrying two coffeepots. The pots smash. I wrote that "the glass pushed into her." I think about the wording now and the way it gave the coffeepots more agency than the human character holding them.

Why did we work there? For me, I think I wanted to put myself in a place where no one would care that I was self-medicating every day, slowly killing myself. A place where I got what I thought I deserved. At Scales, I fit right in. Maybe we all did. Like we were all suffering from the same poison or virus, like we all silently agreed to rules that aren't allowed anywhere else and we lived with them because we knew we were damaged, ruined, not fit for the regular world.

When I try to picture my son's female friends, tiny schoolgirls, growing up to work in a place like that, something breaks open in me. I look into their faces at school events, searching, staring, hoping that no one and nothing is causing them to build the scaffolding inside themselves that would need to be there for them to subject themselves to a place like Scales. I tell myself the world is different now. I know that's mostly a lie.

The EEOC woman named the other waitresses she had spoken to for initial interviews. Almost all of us cooperated. We all said the same thing, the truth of what happened. I thought about trying to reach out to my old coworkers, calling them to talk about the lawsuit, to catch up. But I never did. And they never called me, either. We all said the truth but couldn't say it to each other. Maybe we were afraid to get sucked back into the delusion we used to live with. As if we'd all go back to pretending nothing had happened. And that was something we could no longer live with.

The lawsuit never went anywhere anyway. Soon, I relapsed and was lost again. I didn't have the contact information for the woman from the EEOC. Once I was no longer sober, I had bigger worries. My knees were never the same after spending two years carrying heavy trays up and down the stairs at Scales.

🖎

On the last day of my trip to Chicago with my son, we walked to Ontario Street. I stopped on the sidewalk and stared. The building was gone. There was only green construction fencing and the skeleton of the new high-rise they were building. "New condominiums coming soon! 51 floors of luxury living!" a sign said.

It was like Scales had never been there. I squinted and pictured the old building. I wished I had been there the day they knocked it down. I wished I could have seen the wrecking ball and the rats running for their lives from the building.

I tried to imagine all of us waitresses standing on the sidewalk that day, watching the walls come down, the glass breaking, the dust rising. Maybe we would have had cash in our pockets from new jobs, dollars we would fan out like leaves on a bar somewhere, none of us feeling as relieved as we thought we'd feel, clinking glasses and toasting the demolition.

"Can we go now?" Atlas asked.

I closed my eyes and pictured my old character Bird, standing on the rubble, waving her gun around like a cowgirl, like a gangster, like the chief of police.

"Yes," I told my boy. "We can go now."

The School of the Art Institute of Chicago, 1985.

The School of the Art Institute of Chicago, 2018.

A Steady Yellow Light

A STEADY YELLOW LIGHT tells you a steady red light will soon appear. If you are driving toward an intersection and a yellow light appears, slow down and prepare to stop. If you are within the intersection or cannot stop safely before entering the intersection, continue through carefully.

Department of Transportation, Driver's Manual

YEARS AGO, I ALMOST KILLED SOMEONE ON SACRAMENTO Boulevard in Chicago.

A wide street on the West Side, it cuts through Humboldt Park. I used to drive it once or twice a day like clockwork for months more than two decades ago because it was the fastest path between my apartment and the 24/7 open-air drug market where I shopped back then.

It was late spring and unseasonably warm and I was an addict. On that day, I wore a dressy dry-clean-only dress because all of my clothing was dirty since I hadn't done laundry in a while. My legs stuck to the seats of my dead father's Toyota 4Runner, which I had inherited. I was hot because the air-conditioning was broken and I didn't have the money or the time to get it fixed. The brake pads seemed to be next to go; every stop caused a screeching metal-on-metal noise that embarrassed me more than scared me. One of the guys that I regularly bought from on the corner told me it was the brake pads.

I was sick that day, as I often was between doses back then, and I was sweaty from the heat and my dry-clean-only dress was itchy, and I looked away from the road to fumble with one of the packets I'd just purchased, thinking I could just snort a little at the next light to ease my withdrawal symptoms before going home where I could properly dose myself. And so I was gently opening the paper and holding a rolled-up bill between two fingers of my other hand, the hand that was barely controlling the steering wheel, and I wasn't watching the road, not the way you should be watching a road that runs right through the middle of a city park that was filled with people trying to enjoy the warm weather.

While I was looking down, the light in front of me on the road had changed from green to yellow, so by the time I glanced up again, it was red. I don't know how long it had been red. Long enough for people to begin to cross the intersection. I saw the red light and then immediately saw this young woman rushing quickly toward my car, which made me stomp on my brakes, missing her so narrowly that to this day I think of it as a miracle. I heard the screech of my bad brakes harmonizing with her prolonged scream, and then everything was silent. I held my breath and she slammed her fists down on the hood of my car, her face still holding on to its terrified expression but screaming swear words at me.

When I exhaled, I realized that I had dropped the packet in my lap and checked to make sure I had not spilled the powdered heroin, a reaction that I wish wasn't true. Seeing that the paper had still been folded up enough to protect most of the contents, I looked back at the road and then at the woman, who had made it safely to the other side, where she turned and gave me the finger. It was then that I noticed some kids in the car next to me, teenage guys. It was a two-lane road and they were on my right, in the slow lane. And the driver put his hands out in front of him, palms facing the ground, moving them up and down, like he was saying calm down, chill out. The kid in the passenger seat leaned across his friend, the driver, to yell at me, "What the fuck is wrong with you?"

All these years later, and I still think about how I would not have survived my addiction if I'd hit that woman, and if I had hit her, it would be right for me not to survive it. In recovery meetings, in therapy, in halfway houses, people say only three out of ten addicts survive, and maybe all of us, each one of us sober addicts, have been just one second of bad driving away from not recovering. You do something bad enough, lose your kids out of neglect, burn a house down, sell yourself for drugs, and maybe there isn't enough good left to power through the withdrawal and rebuilding.

Back on Sacramento Avenue that day, I felt my face turning red, hot, and my eyes welling with tears, and all I could think was the answer to that kid yelling at me, *There is so much wrong with me, absolutely everything is wrong with me.*

I turned into the parking area near a small pond and fountain in the park, shaking, too sick to keep driving. I looked all around me to make sure no one was watching and then I pulled at the folds of the package and leaned over it with my rolled dollar bill. I leaned back in my seat and stared out the window.

There was a large crowd in the park, a party, a quinceañera. I wiped at the tears on my face with the heels of my hands.

I could tell which teenage girl the party was for by the way the other girls fawned over her, straightening the train of her dress, carrying her bottled water and her makeup bag, fluffing her hair. Her dress was sleek and fitted up top, with a lower half that broke out into cascading ruffles and tulle.

A photographer was setting up a tripod and camera in front of the crowd of teenagers. Behind the photographer, mothers and aunts and grandmothers in church dresses stood holding their hands over their hearts, tilting their heads, and smiling, draped with the glittery beaded purses of their adolescent offspring.

Waiting to pose with the girls, the teen boys stood nearby in their suits with pastel bow ties and boutonnières. There was a mariachi band, food carts, younger siblings in lacy socks and pat-ent-leather Mary Jane shoes running around and blowing bubbles from little plastic bottles that matched the dresses.

In the spring and summer, there were events like this happening in Humboldt Park all the time. Sometimes there were even wed-dings. I just didn't usually look for long, always rushing through on my daily mission.

I wonder how I had ever turned away from these young people, from adolescence in all its glory, kids playing dress-up convincingly for the first time. Right in front of me, life, people living normal good lives, shadows in my peripheral vision.

Now whenever I see photos of friends' children dressed up for prom or a sweet sixteen party, my first thought is the quinceañera that day in Humboldt Park. One day, I imagine when my son wears a tuxedo for his own prom, waiting for me to take a picture, I will remember again those other teenagers, crying and shaking while watching them, feeling like a ghost seeing the way life is supposed to be.

The woman I almost hit looked to be about my age back then. Maybe now she has a son, too, and maybe she will stand behind a camera one day to photograph him looking so grown-up in his tux. Maybe she will tell him more than once to be careful out there, thinking of me just as often as I think of her.

Street View

Lost Cat, 21 Days Missing
My black/white long-haired cat got out. He has green
eyes and X-large front paws. He could be anywhere. I'm
heartbroken. Please, if anyone sees him, call me.

MY NEIGHBORHOOD, IN NEW HAVEN, CONNECTICUT, HAS A BUSY
online public message board where people ask for plumber recommendations, complain about autumn leaves not being properly bagged, and find each other's lost pets.

The neighborhood borders the harbor and is home to residents who wave to each other and decorate for holidays. In 2018, the real estate website Trulia declared my community one of the top five best areas for Halloween in the country. The East Shore, population 4,567, is a place where you can make the parenting decision to allow your preteen son and his best friend to walk alone to the corner store or to the seawall to hunt for crabs and shells. My son knows the names of all the neighborhood dogs.

Atlas's school is within walking distance of our home, and the crossing guard high-fives every child each morning. There is a family picnic in the fall, a winter dance with a DJ, and a Soap Box Derby in the spring. When I drive down the neighborhood's main road, past the school, the street curves before home and exposes the shining sea. Just past the trees on the hill, it's a view that stuns me each time.

"We are so lucky to live here," I often say to my son.

Door Handles

Guy with a lime green hooded sweater and a backpack on a bicycle in the pouring rain grabbing door handles on Concord Street heading up towards Burr Street now.

After my father died of lung cancer in 1994, during my first attempt at recovery, I sat at his desk in his home office and turned his Rolodex. Under *C* for Cindy, my fingers flipped through card after card filled with my various addresses. In the ten years since I'd left home in Connecticut for college in Chicago, I'd burned through fifteen different apartments.

I wasn't an addict the moment I landed in Chicago in the fall of 1985 to go to art school, but I would have been if someone had met me at baggage claim and folded drugs into the palm of my hand. I could not find meaning in my classes. Living in my own skin was painfully difficult. I didn't eat, couldn't sleep, drank too much. My depressive episodes stacked up month after month, unrelenting, leaving me flailing, hands grasping at anything that would bring momentary relief. When I found heroin, I felt saved. I spent a dozen years renting apartment after apartment through ads in the local free newspaper, circling any awful space I could afford.

When my second husband and I moved to New Haven in 2015, we browsed online. We looked in a few different neighborhoods, but once we saw the East Shore and drove by the seawall, the surface of the water glittery like sequins, we bought the first house we loved.

Mr. Gallo

*Does anyone know what happened in front of Mr. Gallo's
house on Lighthouse? There was a cop car and firetruck and
ambulances. I hope he is OK?*

Addicts like to brag that if dropped into a city, any city, they can
find drugs within the hour. It's a boast that means, *I'm tough enough
to go into this unfamiliar place and secure what I need.* I used to say this
myself, but now that I'm in recovery, I know it's nothing to brag
about. The truth is, it isn't very hard to determine which area of a
city might have drugs for sale.

The neighborhood in Chicago where I used to buy drugs twenty
years ago was West Humboldt Park, or simply the West Side. I
met a man back then who was working a corner, selling drugs to
make extra money to buy Christmas presents for his kids. He told
me where he lived on the West Side, and whenever I couldn't find
someone I trusted to buy from on the streets, I would show up at
his house. He would get drugs for me and I would pay him a small
fee for his trouble. Sometimes I gave his family rides because they
didn't have a car. Their home was always too warm inside, winter
or summer. The living room furniture was covered in plastic to
keep it nice. He and his wife had three boys. The oldest, sixteen,
was a constant source of worry. The second oldest was a preteen,
about the age my son is now.

The mother was pregnant with a fourth child. Once, I gave her a
ride to the government office where she picked up her food stamps.
As I waited in my car, I watched her walk to the double glass doors,
her hands supporting her aching lower back, her belly ballooning
out in front of her, and I was hit by an overwhelming sense of shame.

Stolen Heads

On Alfred Street, near Concord, our huge sunflower heads we were saving for a fall bouquet were expertly taken! Who takes something beautiful we all can enjoy? Getting a new security camera today. :(

Once, when my son was three, I stood on a beach with a group of mothers I didn't know well, and I watched a sweet six-year-old build sandcastles just so my boy could knock them down, again and again. A woman I hadn't met started talking to the other moms about how she was never going to let her addict sister near her children. She made a joke about her sister's disastrous life, and the listeners politely chuckled. I folded my arms and spread my fingers to cover my scars from my own addiction.

When my husband and I moved to New Haven, I stayed quiet about my past, because I felt certain none of the other moms or dads were hiding a background like mine. Then one day I saw a Facebook post from Sherry, the mother of one of my son's friends. She wrote, "Sometimes the thing holding you back is the belief that something is holding you back. Blessed to be in recovery today."

At the third-grade dance in the school cafeteria, when a song came on that Sherry liked, she looked at me and said, "That's my jam!" Then she went on the dance floor and showed the kids how it's done.

I've been watching how the other parents treat Sherry, to see whether they accept her into the community. I'm not proud of this. Even now, more than twenty years after getting clean, I assume people would reject me if they knew—and, more importantly, they would reject my son.

Online, I discovered that Sherry has been clean for about three years. When I hit my three-year mark, I had no children and still woke up every day hoping I wouldn't relapse. In early recovery, no one tells you that it might be a decade or two before you feel truly free from the urge. It has only been in the last few years that I have stopped having dreams about heroin, stopped being brought to my knees by random cravings. Now I have normal dreams like anybody else. Someone is chasing me, my refrigerator is full of live doves when I open the door, I lost my keys again, I have to give a reading in front of a large crowd in nothing but my underwear.

Prank This Morning
We came home this afternoon to find our outside water faucet turned on. Nothing else looks amiss.

The neighborhood message board doesn't tell you whether the person next door has done jail time or gotten a DUI. There are no messages about grown children who live in their parents' basements after stints in rehab. Instead, my neighbors like to post about car break-ins and package theft by assumed outsiders. Some of them include grainy security videos of people in hoodies or ball caps pulling at car door handles. Once, a video showed the street I live on and three figures moving past my car in the dark. I do not feel the same outrage as my neighbors about this. Instead I ask myself: Would I have broken into people's cars twenty years ago? Sick from withdrawal, would I have followed UPS trucks on their delivery routes and then stolen the packages they left on front porches? In recovery, they say that anything terrible you haven't done is simply a "yet" if you don't find sobriety.

Watching my neighbors' videos of suspected criminals made me want to see the West Side again, if only through pictures.

I look up my last apartment building on Google Maps, then select Street View. Clicking the mouse to move down the street, I take the same drive I used to take twice a day. Click, click, click. There is the underpass that marks the beginning of the West Side, like the border between two countries. Click, click. There's the old Popeye's Chicken, still open for business after two decades.

My past is right where I left it.

The Google Street View images are taken by cameras mounted on cars, then the images are stitched together to form an endless panorama. You can see people on the sidewalks, kids jumping rope, crossing guards in their neon vests, one white-gloved hand holding back traffic while children move across an intersection. Illicit acts have also been captured on Street View—everything from public urination to muggings. Had Street View existed twenty years ago, I might have been caught on camera getting out of my car or moving toward the corner boys like a ghost. Like the figures filmed by my neighbors' security cameras, I would have yanked my hood forward to hide my face.

Trash Left on Pope Street

My husband & I have been picking up trash that has been left on our lawn on the right side of Pope St. by a parent that takes their child to the elementary school. It's always from McDonald's. Too lazy to put in trash pail in front of school. What are they teaching their children. They should be ashamed of themselves.

It is strange to be on the other side, a member of the readership for neighborhood complaints instead of the subject of a neighborhood complaint. If there had been an online message board for the West Side all those years ago, would the neighbors have photographed my license plate and talked about how sick they were of these white people showing up on their streets and buying drugs in the open, as if they had a right to? *Don't they even care if kids see? Don't they care about how they are helping to destroy the neighborhood?*

As I continue my virtual journey through the West Side, I see a few young men sitting on milk crates or leaning against fences. The corner boys always had an uncanny ability to melt into the shadows when necessary, slipping in and out of view like spirits.

There is a high that comes from the act of buying drugs. The ritual of driving to the West Side would make my heart beat faster and my palms sweat. A giddiness would come over me. Just seeing it again on my computer screen, I feel a nervous electricity down to my fingertips.

Street View shows me block after block of pawnshops, storefront churches, used furniture stores, liquor stores, corner markets selling lottery tickets, ramen noodles, and cigarettes. When I see young men standing together on a corner, I lean in, my face inches from the screen: Was this one of my spots? Would I recognize their blurry faces? As if I ever really looked at them to begin with.

Coyote vs. Cat
There were two coyotes laying under a tree on my lawn on
Lighthouse Rd. at 3 am. I watched for a few minutes as one

paced back and forth and all of a sudden a cat fell from the tree. Sadly, the cat didn't get away. The cat looked like it had dark fur and white paws. Please keep your pets inside.

I click left down Hamlin Street, each frame melting into the next. Was this the block where I'd seen the most violent beating I'd ever witnessed? I had been parked under a tree at midday, trying to discreetly snort a little heroin to stave off withdrawal before driving home. I was bent over the powder with a clipped straw when the screams made me straighten up. A crew of teens had surrounded a kid who was maybe thirteen at most. They fell on the boy without the slightest pause. I'll never forget the awful thudding as they kicked him.

I wish I could say that I got out of my car, or at least rolled down my window and yelled at them to stop. But I simply sat there watching, sick to my stomach in a jittery, clammy way that had nothing to do with withdrawal.

An old woman in a station wagon saved him. She screeched to a stop at the intersection, jumped out, and hit the boys with a cane. The teens took their time walking away from the crumpled body in the street, as if to let her know they weren't leaving because of her; they were just finished, that's all. She stood her ground until they turned their backs. When she helped the boy up, a bloody string of mucus stretched from his head to the street.

Chickens Killed
Just wanted to share a heads up that 2 of my chickens have been killed here on Townsend Avenue. Of course, my two favorites! Has anybody noticed increased predator activity lately?

The oldest son of that family I knew on the West Side got arrested once. His parents had always told him that they'd beat his ass if they found him on the corner selling drugs, even though his father sometimes did. They made him sit at the table every night and do his homework because they wanted a better life for him. But he was sixteen and didn't listen.

After his arrest, I drove his mom to the courthouse. Her face was swollen from crying. When her son was finally brought into the courtroom in handcuffs, his eyes scanned the rows for his mom. I could see the fear in his face, and his comfort the minute he spotted her: here was a child who needed his mother. What I didn't see was how I contributed to the environment that had made it so tempting for him to work a corner. I didn't worry about what those kids saw on the West Side.

Those kids are now in their twenties and thirties. What if they googled my current neighborhood on Street View? Would they see my son and his friends on their bikes and scooters? Instead of boys on the corner, they might see the mailman, or the teenager who cuts our grass, or me on the front steps, laptop balanced on my knees, glass of iced tea next to me.

When I was sweating it out in rehab, throwing up, bedsheets stuck to my skin, legs restless, I did not know exactly the life I would have after I got sober, but I imagined something infinitely better than the life I had been living. I could count on that without even thinking about it. I would have job opportunities, access to higher education, money, a safety net, a quiet neighborhood. Would I have stopped using if I'd thought there might not be anything better for me?

Complaints

Good evening neighbors, the complaining in this neighborhood has to come to a minimum. Let's be grateful that we have amazing views. It's a little piece of tranquility tucked away. I get saddened by how people seem to forget how good we really have it. Every neighborhood has its problems. I think ours are small compared to most.

Click, click, click. I turn right onto Huron and move down the block. I take a right at Harding. Here is their block. There is the house of the family I knew, second-to-last from the stop sign. I pivot to the left until I have a straight-on view of the home. That family let me in even when it was late at night; they never turned me away. The weeds are tall by the steps. The windows are covered with plywood. No one seems to live there now. They've moved on to someplace better. At least, I hope so.

Self-Storage

Lessor agrees to lease the storage unit on a month-to-month basis. The Lessee shall pay a security deposit of one month's rent due upon signing with each month's rent thereafter due on or before the 15th.

1 My high school yearbook, Cheshire High School, Class of 1985. A Cat Stevens quote, a serious photo of me looking off into the distance, as if I would never be the kind of person who would have to put everything I owned into storage in order to enter rehab.

2 A Raggedy Ann doll, a gift when I was little, made for me by a friend of my mother's, who embroidered "I love Cindy" inside a heart on the doll's chest, hidden beneath her calico dress.

3 Deer antlers mounted on a wooden plaque, along with the arrow that had killed the animal. On the shaft of the arrow, a label written by my dead father: our last name in capital letters. Every summer, my dad would come home from work, change out of his suit, and shoot arrows into a target attached to a haystack in the backyard, practicing for deer season in the fall. *Thwack* was the sound of the

arrows hitting the target, and then he would walk over to pull them out and start again.

This is a friendly reminder that your rent has not been received and is past due. If this was an oversight, please send your payment immediately in order to avoid any late charges. Thank you for your prompt attention to this matter.

4 A photo of a boy I loved when I was a teenager; he was standing in front of a lake, hands in the pockets of his khakis, navy blazer unbuttoned, loafers and no socks. He died young and without a photo of me anywhere in his effects, I am sure.

5 A hummingbird, carved out of wood by my father during the last years of his life.

6 A folder with photos of the art I made in high school. A wall sculpture I made from wood fragments, wire, and paper, inspired by a front-page image in the *New Haven Register* of corroded city pipes.

7 The CD of a band whose lead singer had been an old boyfriend. Before I left for college, he had given me two books that made me want to write: *Black Tickets* by Jayne Anne Phillips and *Trilobites* by Breece D'J Pancake. Years later, I went to see his band at Avalon Nightclub on Belmont in Chicago. We were surprised to discover that we were both high.

This notice is to inform you that we have made several attempts to collect outstanding rent due. Please be advised that if collection is required, your debt obligation will increase due to court costs, attorney's fees, interest, and other related costs that may be incurred.

8 A letter from my best friend in high school, quoting at length from Rilke's *Letters to a Young Poet*, her earnest handwriting filling the pages.

9 A sea-foam-green velvet sofa, purchased on a Chicago street for fifty dollars, and moved from one apartment to another over the years.

10 A pair of pants made for me by a friend in the Fashion Department at the School of the Art Institute of Chicago. They were sewn from scraps of leftover fabric she had used for other projects, squares of crisp cotton, almost shiny. Sometimes I can picture them hanging in my closet now, right there for me to grab and slide into.

11 A large painting made by one of my first close friends in college, a Bible glued facedown in the middle of dark green and red paint, like a murder in a forest church.

12 A music box made for me by the boyfriend I started using with, when he was clean and I was not, a last present, a goodbye. The wood pieces were sanded and built around a windup steel mechanism, called a movement, that played the song "Row, Row, Row Your Boat." On the lid of the music box, the boyfriend had placed a photo he'd taken of me, sitting on a counter, arms wrapped around my knees to hide my lack of clothing, staring at the camera and smiling.

You have failed to pay rent for storage of personal property. Pursuant to IL Stats70490, the operator of this self-service storage facility is allowed to deny you access to your personal property until you pay the operator all rent and other charges due. This is your second notice of default.

13 A Mac desktop computer from the mid-nineties, when most people I knew did not have a home computer. It was the property of a brilliant man I lived with in D.C. and still feel bad about because I don't think he knew how troubled I was or what he was getting himself into. When we broke up, I kept his computer, which is to say I stole it, and he didn't deserve that, especially when it ended up being abandoned in storage anyway. He'd had an emotional affair with another woman, which is how I justified keeping his computer.

14 Paper copies of all of the short stories I'd written in my twenties, a dozen or so, maybe more, and they were my only copies, since back then I wrote everything on a typewriter.

You are being asked to leave the premises. If you are in doubt regarding your legal rights and obligations as a tenant, it is recommended that you seek legal assistance. This entire balance must be paid immediately. In the event you elect not to pay the rental and late charge, consider this a notice of eviction.

☛

I have another list now, things I would never abandon. A plaster mold of my son's hand when he was three and a lock of his soft shiny hair from his first haircut, my framed master's degree, a bracelet from my husband with the word home engraved on the part of the metal that touches my skin, drawings my father made as a teenager, now framed on the wall of my office. They don't replace the lost things. If you shake me, the past still rattles around inside. I close my eyes and an old zipper from a favorite pair of pants shivers over my skin. The weightlessness of a wooden hummingbird sits in my palm. Old letters twist and stretch themselves out of their envelopes like snakes shedding their skin, revealing loopy, girlish handwriting that says I want you to live, please survive this.

The Roof over Our Heads

WE MOVED IN WITH WHAT WE COULD CARRY. SOME OF US HAD A suitcase, a cardboard box, a garbage bag full of emptied drawers. Some of us had nothing but the clothing on our bodies and a hospital bracelet still strangling a wrist.

We filled out forms and signed contracts, a promise to abide by the rules, a pledge to stay clean and go to meetings, an agreement to submit to random drug tests when asked.

We were shown to a specific apartment, a room, and then to a twin bed that we could say was ours. It was a U-shaped building in a neighborhood at the edge of the city, a few blocks' walk from the last train stop. There was nothing to identify it as a residence for addicts and we liked it that way. To each other, we called it a recovery house, but to the outside world, we just called it the place where we lived. We pretended it was a building tenanted like any other in the city, its residents chosen by their ability to produce the first and last month's rent.

I arrived at the beginning of summer, the weather already uncomfortably humid. I came straight from O'Hare Airport after a stint in a Connecticut rehab hospital. I wanted to be back in Chicago and I didn't have a lot of options. I'd made the arrangements over the phone. I was puffy and pale, bloated from a cocktail of prescribed psychotropic drugs to manage my chronic depression, exacerbated by the anhedonia of new recovery.

The apartment was filled with scarred secondhand furniture. I sat in front of the box fan in the window of my assigned room, at the end of the bare mattress of the twin bed I would sleep on. My roommate was at a meeting. My bags were at my feet. I let the fan blow the hair off my sweaty face.

❧

Only a handful of residents in the building were in therapy. Most of the people I knew in recovery turned to free AA/NA meetings and some kind of halfway house where there was a requirement to stay sober. We paid rent for amenities like a chore requirement and the expectation of a drug test should we come home stumbling, slurring, not ourselves. There was a director who collected rent and ran a monthly community meeting, and those with seniority received a rent reduction for watching over the rest of us.

Some called it a halfway house and others preferred recovery house. We were halfway to somewhere else, somewhere new, as if we could not bear to step all the way in. Addiction wasn't a whole life, not a real life, but without it, I was hard-pressed to say what my whole life might be. I lived a halfway life, in a halfway house, with a halfway job I hated, gritting my teeth through halfway days.

❧

We needed jobs and lives, things to fill our free time once we stopped using, a way to support ourselves and pay off our substantial debts. We filled out employment applications and waited for phone calls.

During my interview at a little storefront restaurant just west of the Gold Coast, the owner sat across from me holding a tiny sleeping beagle puppy in the palm of his hand. He wanted someone to run the restaurant so he could spend his time opening two more. He said he remembered me from a year ago when I'd worked the door at my friend's new hot-spot restaurant in River West. I had been charming, he said. *I must have been high that shift*, I thought.

"His name is Flambé," the owner said, looking down at the dog in his hand.

Over his shoulder, I stared at a line of awful paintings hung over an upholstered banquette down one side of the restaurant. He followed my gaze and looked behind him.

"Who made the paintings?" I asked, knowing the answer.

"I did," he said. "I'm kind of an all-around artist-slash-creative person. I'm not just a chef."

Flambé yawned with his eyes closed.

"When can you start?" the owner asked.

 ✒

We went to meetings. We said the slogans and circled up and held hands. It worked if we worked it. We collected and compared our sobriety coins and didn't mind that they were plastic, that they never jingled in our pockets when we walked.

I mostly went to the meetings in our building because it was convenient, but my favorite meeting, when I could make it, was on Sheffield. That meeting was full of people with lives I wanted to hear about. A photographer, a detective, a clothing designer. I felt glamour wafting off the designer, as if he hadn't paid the price the rest of us had paid for our addictions. My life was so dreary, colorless. I assumed nothing would ever be fun again, but this designer was still living a life that sparkled.

The meetings in our building were sadder. They were held in

the basement, where it smelled like smoke and something gamey. An odor similar to the smell in my childhood garage after my father had strung up a dead deer at the end of a cold November day during hunting season. I couldn't figure out why it would smell like that beneath the ground in a recovery house in a major city.

I was one of the few who had a job; the room was full of people worried about bills they couldn't pay, needing things they couldn't afford. The designer from my preferred meeting in that hipper neighborhood had expensive new shoes every month, but in the basement room I was the lucky one with money in my pocket and nice clothes for work. It was hard to be called lucky when I felt sure I'd never feel good again, but I knew it was true.

Even though we knew each other from living under the same roof, we still started everything we said with, "Hi, I'm Cindy and I'm an addict." It added to the misery of the room somehow, as if we were saying we couldn't be bothered to remember each other's names. It was like we were admitting that we would never know or be known, that we were all just passing through completely alone.

It was that room of people that I told first about my new job.

"Why do you sound like someone killed your dog if you just got a job?" a woman named Jasmine asked.

"Why don't *you*?" I said back. "Don't you feel like your dog died? Doesn't everyone here feel like they have a dead dog?"

✌

We did chores. They were part of the rules and the contract for living in the building. I understood right away that if I wanted even a baseline acceptance from the rest of the community, I'd have to do my chores not just as well as most people, but even a little better.

I was one of only a handful of white people living in the building. They called me Princess the day I came in and that seemed fair, the idea that I was guilty of being a spoiled entitled asshole until I could prove myself something closer to relatable. I came to them off a plane from Connecticut, wearing good clothes with family paying my rent for that first month. They weren't wrong about who they thought I might be.

I wasn't part of the "we" when I arrived, and even now I hesitate when I type it. I have no right to speak for them. We were a "we" because we all shared the same faulty coping skills that we worked to shed. And no one wants to be alone while shedding the only thing that made it feel okay to be alive.

I did my chores to rap music like everybody else. In that building, our recoveries were fueled by rap. The building breathed it from the windows, and sometimes you could know who was struggling more than usual by song choice and volume. So many rap songs speak to accomplishing the impossible and have this mix of joy and anger that works well, an anthem of fighting and clawing your way to a life people assumed you'd never have.

It was so long ago that I listened to music on a Walkman with cassette tapes. I polished the banisters in the hallways with Tupac singing "Keep Ya Head Up" in my ears.

I was embarrassed when I felt the music; it was music that didn't belong to me. I was mortified to be seen feeling anything, good or bad. I would focus on the movements I had to make to clean, not wanting anyone to see my head nodding along to the beat even though they couldn't hear it.

Mopping the floors in the basement community room with Digable Planets singing "Rebirth of Slick (Cool Like Dat)" in my ears, I did my best to look like someone not feeling a beat, not feeling a thing.

❧

Out in the world—at our jobs, on dates, with family—we kept secret our bad luck and our bad behavior. If we had needle scars, we pulled our sleeves down. If we'd found violence in our addiction, we smiled with our lips pressed together, hiding missing teeth. But when we came home to the recovery house, we hid our *good* luck. We minimized our positive news. The good became the secret. Some of us didn't want to rub it in. Some of us didn't want to advertise the amount of steady money we were earning. Some of us were afraid we'd jinx it by saying it out loud.

After a long shift at the restaurant and the train ride north to the last stop, I'd come home on sore feet to a mostly quiet building. The curfew was ten p.m. and I'd arrive after midnight, when most people had gone to bed, having nothing better to do. I had special permission to be out late because I worked a night job.

In my apartment, in my room, I'd change out of my work clothes while my roommate snored. She took antidepressants that had a side effect of sleepiness, Trazodone, a drug they often prescribed for addicts, as it was nonhabit-forming, and she wore an eye mask and headphones playing white noise, as if she were courting the feeling of being dead once the sun went down. I'd try to be quiet anyway as I slipped the wad of cash I'd earned inside my pillowcase for the night. The restaurant owner had me pay myself from the drawer when I did the day's receipts. Every shift closing would bring me to the same thought. *This money would be such a trigger if I was close to relapsing.* A lie I told myself because we were all close to relapsing, every day, and the triggers remained triggers whether we named them or not.

🙢

We were never alone, never had enough personal space, and yet, in our crowded building, apartments, rooms, we were each so lonely.

We were told not to look for romantic relationships, not to date. We didn't listen. Almost everyone wanted to be with almost anyone. We weren't picky. We had holes inside to fill, places vast and wide, plains where we could imagine the wind whistling, hauntings from the ghosts of the substances that had been our true loves. I ached for my high. I would have filled that spot with anything or anyone I thought had a shot at taking my mind off it.

"That white boy is looking at you all the time," my roommate, Rayelle, said. "He keeps them rats in his room. I don't know how that's even allowed."

She was talking about Davis and his pet ferrets. Sometimes he walked them on leashes in the courtyard. Rayelle always went inside when she saw them.

"They bite," I told her.

"Is that a white people thing?" she said.

"A white *boy* thing, maybe," I said.

She was right. Davis looked at me often. I decided I would sleep with him because it seemed easy. He was right there.

🙢

We wanted things in a way that was different from normal people and we could smell this on each other. Food, sex, material possessions that would prove we were worth something. Our eyes shifted left and right, always looking for a way to get what we needed. I had this even as a kid, probably all of us did. Seeing it now in kids I know, a couple of my son's friends, makes me shiver, just picturing their future, the desperation that kind of want can grow into, the way a kid's unmet needs can take over the rest of his life.

One day in the courtyard, I noticed Davis staring at me. I'd lost anything resembling nuance in my addiction. Like someone coming back from a near-death experience, I didn't have time or energy to invest in subtlety.

"You and I should just sleep together already," I said to him.

He narrowed his eyes and stared at me through the smoke of the cigarette he held frozen in front of his mouth. "Wow," he said.

"Wow, what?"

"I'm just shocked."

"What the fuck, Davis?" I said. "Yes or no?"

"Yeah, totally yeah."

꒜

In our dreams, we did our drugs, we returned to the scenes of our crimes, we snorted and shot and smoked and thought, *Oh god, finally, where have you been?* And then we woke up, devastated and blinking in the daylight of sobriety.

Davis and I ended up in the faded lobby of a crappy motel on the Northwest Side. Even as I pulled my license and cash out, I vowed to forget that it was I who paid. Davis sprang that on me at the last minute and it embarrassed me, but I still pulled out my wallet. We were already there, standing on dirty shag carpeting in a smoky lobby, the old man at the front desk comparing me to the photo on my license.

In the room, there was a pilled bedspread on the bed, which dipped low in the middle. The only light was a buzzing overhead fluorescent, making everything uglier and harsher. Rust stained the sink under the faucet in the bathroom.

Davis kept bragging about how he never had any trouble with erections all through his addiction, so proud of it.

"Well, I wasn't thinking about fucking at all in my addiction, so I wouldn't have given a shit whether your dick worked or not, only if you had money or drugs. But good for you," I said.

"I'm just saying," Davis said. "Most guys have a lot of problems in that area when they're fucked up."

"So you've been with a lot of dudes who couldn't get it up for you?"

During the actual act, I had a clear moment of thinking that the next time I stupidly believed I could replace my beloved heroin, I would skip this shit and go right to jelly donuts.

And then I was picking my bra off the floor, buttoning my jeans, checking the time, rushing out of the room, lonelier than I'd been when I got there. And more worried because I would have to see Davis and his stupid ferrets every goddamn day in the courtyard of my own fucking building.

꒰

Our lives were compartmentalized. When we recognized each other in our regular routines out in the world, we froze. Like secret agents, we would read the scene to choose whether to say hello or not. Most of us had at least one scenario where we needed to not be asked, "How do you two know each other?"

One day, I saw Nick, a regular at the Sheffield meeting, on a street downtown. He was a detective and I'd heard his stories about taking drugs from the evidence room, about his wife leaving him, about almost losing his job.

I watched him slam a guy over the hood of his car and handcuff him. He was out of breath, pressing on the man's back to keep him pinned to the car. His partner was running down the sidewalk to get to him and Nick looked once over his shoulder to see how close he was and when he turned back, our eyes met. We both just stared for a moment and then I broke the spell by looking away and crossing to the other side of the street as if I didn't know Nick at all. It stayed with me all day, seeing Nick that way. I'd never fully imagined him doing his work. I never pictured what it might be like arresting criminals when you knew you were capable of your own illegal behavior.

☙

We all had these tests and each one mattered so much. Failing them could equal our plunge back into addiction. In equal measure, we feared and longed for that failure.

The court date returning our children from foster care, the job interview, the spouse who would or would not take us back, the driving suspension lifted, the forgiveness of our families granted. We waited and hoped and shoved our plan B, total relapse, into the back of our minds. For now.

I focused on work. I cleaned out the storage closet in the basement of the restaurant, dusting off cases of wine and relabeling everything. It was a mess, with random bottles that weren't even on our wine list anymore. One day I went around to the advertising agencies in the neighborhood with a basket of cookies the chef had made and a coupon for a discount on large work parties. I made the schedule for the waitstaff and I hired a hostess. I functioned.

One night a couple by the window made a waitress cry. The man had a coupon that we no longer accepted. I would have just given him the lousy ten percent off the bill, but he opened his mouth the second I got to the table.

"I'm not putting up with your bullshit, too," he said.

"I beg your pardon?"

"You people," he said, pointing at me. "You use this promotional shit to get people in here and then you refuse to honor it. You're fucking dishonorable."

I felt my face getting hot.

There were nights I had driven into the drug neighborhood with an energy shimmering off me, and when I imagined the possibility of getting ripped off as I sometimes was, I was sure I could kill someone. I'd started buying on those corners with fear sitting in my chest, and by the end of my addiction I felt like I could easily murder someone just for selling me talcum powder. In all the weeks of being clean, I hadn't felt that rage again, not until now, staring at that guy spitting out those words at me.

"If you'd looked it up, you would've seen that we're no longer participating in that promotion. So, no, I'm not honoring your coupon. Now, how would you like to pay?"

I pictured throwing the table over, spilling their drinks and the bread basket, screaming from my core, the place where I was furious that I had to live that way, sober every minute for as long as I lived.

And then I had a craving that made me break out into a sweat. A craving that made the room go dark, made my hands clench into vibrating fists.

"Fuck you," the man said.

I took a deep breath and looked at the woman who sat with him, but she wouldn't meet my eyes. The room got quiet and people at the nearby tables, I realized, were all staring.

"Excuse me," I whispered.

I went behind the bar and put my hand around the neck of a Grey Goose bottle while dialing the phone with my other hand. I wasn't sure if I wanted to drink it or smash it. I called the silent partner who lived in the apartment above the restaurant. He worked in IT and sometimes came down for a beer at the end of the night, but he left the day-to-day operations to his friend the chef. His hobby was weight lifting, and although he always offered to come down if needed, I'd never had to call him before.

"Can you please come down here right now? There's a problem customer."

I wiped the bar down and let the owner handle it. He made the man leave and he brought me the credit card receipt he'd forced him to sign. On the line where the tip should have gone, the man had written, *FUCK YOU*.

I pulled my wallet out of my purse and handed the server a twenty-dollar bill for her tip.

How was I going to stay sober in a world like this? How were any of us staying sober?

≈

We looked for ways we could make dramatic changes to our lives, anything to alter the reality of who we had been. Sometimes we made choices that we knew went against recovery rules, but we told ourselves we were different.

I imagined a curtain, a wisp of fabric I could pass through to get to the alternate reality of my life, the life I would have lived, should have been living, if not for my addiction. As if addiction had been some random accident, a thing that happened *to* me, a bump in the road that could not be helped. As if I could just pass through the curtain and watch it blowing in the breeze behind me.

I started circling ads for studio apartments, telling myself I was fine and didn't need the recovery house anymore. At night, coming home on the train after work, I scribbled in my notebook and pretended I was writing again.

When Kendra and Darnell announced in a basement meeting that they were getting married, we were quick to say congrats, to act like it was normal and fine, a sound decision. Except for Rayelle, who could never pretend.

"I can't believe you all are encouraging this," she said to the rest of us.

"Can't you be happy for us?" Kendra asked.

"You got maybe three months' clean time combined, the both of you," Rayelle said. "Come on, now, don't act like you don't know this isn't putting your sobriety first. Girl, please."

Darnell jerked his chair a couple of inches closer to Kendra's and put his arm around her.

"And Darnell," Rayelle said. "You just got here and you already engaged to someone in this house. Lord help me. Don't act like you're protecting her, comforting her from the big meanie in the room. If you gave a shit about her or yourself, you wouldn't be doing this."

And then she stood up and threw her soda can hard into the garbage near the door before slamming her way out and up the stairs.

We all knew she was right but no one said another word. We closed the meeting and went our separate ways in the building.

﹌

Sometimes we watched our peers struggle and relapse. We told ourselves this was part of the process. We helped the relapsers pack their things and we hugged them before they left. Sometimes we told ourselves that wouldn't be us. Sometimes we wished it was us.

If the news was that a person in recovery attempted suicide, it meant it wasn't a relapse. They'd tried to die using other means. If they attempted suicide by purposely overindulging in their drug of choice, then the other addicts would call it "attempted suicide" with air quotes. Because even if the person had ended up dead or close to dead, in the early moments of that decision we all understood that it was a relief or even a joy, at least in the beginning.

It was Davis's roommate that everyone was gossiping about in the courtyard one afternoon when I got home from the dry cleaner's.

Wade had not been liked by most of us. He wore ties every day and gave out unsolicited advice. He talked too much at meetings.

They said he had drunk antifreeze and probably wasn't going to survive. He was in the ICU downtown. His coworkers found him in his office at the end of the day, seizing under his desk.

Maybe it was a comforting thought for him to die by drinking something toxic. I'd never heard of anyone trying to kill himself with antifreeze before.

As soon as I heard people saying hell no, they wouldn't be visiting that motherfucker, I decided I had to go. It just seemed too sad to picture him in his hospital bed in the ICU with no visitors. Had

I been seeing a therapist at that time, we could have discussed the way I always felt responsible for how other people felt, like I had to somehow fix the cruelties in their lives.

At Northwestern Memorial, I sat in a hard plastic chair next to Wade, who had been blinded from the antifreeze. I went there thinking I was this savior, this rescuer, and he kept saying, "I just don't remember you. What was your name again?" He might have remembered me if he could have seen my face, but still, it was so typical of the kind of asshole he'd always been. I knew everyone's name in the building. What kind of a crappy person can't even place the name once he's reminded? Then I wondered if he had brain damage. It's not a question I could have asked him. The sympathy came rushing back. *This poor bastard*, I thought, looking at him helpless and hooked up to tubes and monitors in his hospital bed.

Finally, I thought enough time had gone by where it would be okay to leave. I said I had to get to work, which wasn't true but I wanted to get out of there.

"Thanks for coming by, Sandy," Wade said.

꙳

Kendra and Darnell's wedding took place in the courtyard at the end of the summer. I had to work and I hoped they'd serve the giant grocery store sheet cake before I had to leave.

Some of the women in the house had gone to the Goodwill superstore in the neighborhood to help Kendra find her dress. Rayelle refused to take part in any of the planning or celebrating and Kendra had stopped speaking to her. The last time I saw them talk, it had ended with Kendra screaming, "I'm grown!"

Justus, the director of the house, was officiating, which surprised Rayelle and made her want to move to another recovery house.

"He's supposed to help us stay clean," she complained in the privacy of our room one night.

She had a point, but she was being so rigid that it was hard to be around her. The rest of us were tired of the rules and deprivation. We needed to celebrate something. We needed to see someone get what they thought they wanted.

People were carrying folding chairs up from the basement meeting room and setting them in rows in the courtyard. It was good it hadn't rained because the grass in the courtyard had worn away to dirt and even a brief shower always turned it to mud.

Justus stood in the middle of the activity, notecards in his hand. He was wearing a suit, which I'd never seen him wear before. I took a seat.

Davis slipped in beside me.

"You should at least take off your baseball cap," I said.

"I didn't see on the invite that this was black tie. Sorry—not everyone has the money to get all decked out like you."

"Davis, I'm going to work. I dress like this for work because I'm supposed to wear this at work. You know, work, a job, work."

"I'm just messing with you," he said. "When we hooking up again?"

"We're not."

❧

We were used to being eyed suspiciously, but still we were outraged when falsely accused. Outraged in a way that now seems comical. I mean, we were all capable of it, so why feel so insulted? Every last one of us was so close to a slip every day.

Rayelle found an almost-empty bottle of vodka behind the couch in our apartment one night. There were only four of us living in our two-bedroom apartment and the other two roommates were hardly ever home, plus they had more seniority, so I must have seemed like the obvious owner of the bottle.

"Is this yours?" she said when I came in, standing at the door, swinging it by the neck casually in one hand, like she'd been standing there all night waiting for me to get home.

"Of course it's not mine," I said. "What the hell? It's not even my drug of choice."

I pushed past her and went into our room, Rayelle following close behind. She shut the door behind her and sat on her bed, holding the vodka bottle on her lap.

"You can tell me," she said. "I'm trying to help you."

"Oh my god, Rayelle," I said. "I have been on my feet for the last nine hours, dealing with horrible people treating dinner like it's an emergency, and I don't need your crap right now. Please."

"I just don't see any other explanation. You were the only one up last night. Maybe you just stashed it behind the couch and forgot about it."

"I want you to think very carefully about what happened in this apartment during all these hours when I was gone. I already answered you—it's not mine."

"You know what I just remembered?" she said. "Tasha had that girl over, the one who wants to come live here. And I left for my meeting. Shoot, my bad."

"Can you get out of my face now? This shit is ridiculous."

I sat down on my bed and slipped my heels off. Rayelle stood over me, her eye mask dangling at her neck, huge fluffy bathrobe cinched at the waist, slippers on her feet, hair wrapped up in a silk scarf. She looked like someone's mother on a bad sitcom.

"Girl, don't be all mad," she said. "It's not like it's impossible that it could've been you."

~

We struggled with holidays and how to get through them sober. They made us feel like freaks. We felt excluded. A holiday could derail an addict's sobriety in seconds. Tradition had a way of reminding us where we went wrong and forcing us to stare at people who seemed to have done everything right.

The first holiday in my sobriety that year was Halloween. Rayelle and most of the people in the house talked me into meeting them at a sober event after work.

I set the night alarm, locked the restaurant, and looked for a cab. It had been dead and I got out at a reasonable time. There was an autumn chill in the air and the streets were filled with grown-ups in costumes, drunk, laughing, stumbling by me.

In the cab, I stared out the window as we drove north. I missed having a car. I missed my old life, not the end of my addiction when things had gotten out of hand, but before that, when I had friends and drank in bars like a normal person. I always drank more than the people around me and I always had trouble stopping but it wasn't the problem that it became once I moved to heroin. I missed being able to think about getting drunk when the day was bad, missed having something to offer myself when I thought I couldn't cope.

At the dance, I pushed through the crowd, looking for anyone from my house. I saw Rayelle in a corner, holding a grape soda and dancing like she was holding back.

"You made it," she said. "Where's your costume?"

"I'm dressed like a restaurant manager," I told her. I looked down at the black dress I'd worn to work. "Or a widow."

She had on a pair of cat ears and a tail but the rest of her outfit was everyday Rayelle, jeans and a hoodie and Jordans.

In the middle of the room, there was a dance floor with a DJ and strobe lights. A large group of people were in formation doing the Electric Slide. Davis jumped in and added himself to the end of the front row. I looked at Rayelle and she laughed. She made eye contact with a couple of women from the third floor who were on the dance floor and they all cracked up. One of them imitated Davis's moves when he couldn't see. I felt bad for Davis then, not because I had any feelings for him, but just because I didn't know the Electric Slide, either. And because without a drink, I wouldn't have even attempted it.

They say in recovery you're frozen right at the age you were when you first picked up. You stop growing emotionally because you never learn to work through anything. We were like a room full of middle school kids. Making fun of each other, drinking too much soda, or hugging the wall like our peers might bite us. I stood there feeling thirteen again, every bit as awkward and friendless and alone as I was back then.

❧

We longed to be worth something again. We wanted to be seen as trustworthy, honest, good, anything besides who we had been in our addiction. The path back seemed so long, so hard, and we didn't always walk it in the right way.

The restaurant where I worked was right on the edge of the Gold Coast, near galleries, a few ad agencies. Just a few blocks away was some of the most extreme poverty in the entire city.

Two kids, sisters, came in one day in the middle of the afternoon, between the lunch and dinner rushes. I was restocking the bar. They wanted to know if I would buy candy for a school fundraiser. I bought their whole box that day. I had money and I thought I could give the candy out at the next basement meeting. Then I gave them free sodas at the bar and chatted with them. They were young, maybe eight and ten years old.

I was thinking about the family whose dad would get me what I needed when I had trouble finding it, and how his kids knew why I was there. I buried any guilt I had about those kids because my need was my priority back then.

These sisters had nothing to do with that. And when they came in the next day and the next, asking me for soda—and why wouldn't they?—my boss told me to tell them they couldn't come back. And I did that, I told them to stop coming in. Which was far worse than if I'd just bought a single candy bar that first day and escorted them out. I didn't know how to be good to people without overdoing it, how to just be a person in the world.

🖝

The figure we all repeated often was this: only three out of ten addicts recover. Even today in recovery literature, you can find the statistic that thirty percent recover, but there is nothing about what they base this number on. I wonder why I didn't ask more questions. Where did this number come from? And what was meant by recover? Recovery is always an ongoing process with no end because an addict can relapse at any time, so how exactly were they defining the recovery of these three out of ten? Is it a decade of being clean? Two decades? Until they die of natural causes?

I relapsed on a normal day, after living in the house for about six months. I wish I could say it happened because someone died, or I got fired, or some other awful thing occurred. But the truth is I just thought of using one day like I always thought about it and instead of telling myself no and moving on to the next thing, I said, *Yes. Why not? I'm sick of this. One time won't kill me. I've been good.*

I was at the restaurant, setting up for the dinner shift. One of the busboys who was working that night had a car and I asked to borrow it. Admitting this is worse than admitting the relapse. This guy worked so hard and he needed his car for his second job making deliveries during the day. He needed to earn money to send back to his wife and kids in Mexico. Whenever I needed someone to pick up an extra shift, he came in for me. And I risked his livelihood and I made that choice while sober.

It is one of the things I will think of now in my present life, out of the blue, just right in the middle of my day, and feel my face growing hot from shame.

But on that day, I didn't care. I left the restaurant, claiming I had an emergency and would be right back, and then I went back to the neighborhood I had once gone to every day. I found someone on a corner and I traded cash for little packages and felt the first excitement and anticipation I'd felt in months.

I went back to the restaurant and somehow got through the dinner shift without touching it but then as the evening wound down and we only had a few tables left in the dining room, I locked myself in the office alone.

Rayelle led one of the basement meetings and I'd try to attend to show support. Many times, there would be new people who had just shown up at the house and didn't know all the rules yet. In meetings, you aren't supposed to give detailed accounts of when you used or what it was like or how it felt. It could lead people to relapse and no one needed to hear about that. Whenever someone would start down that path, not realizing it was frowned upon, Rayelle would say, "Hold up, hold up, hold up. We don't need no crackalogue." And she would cut them off.

I could talk about the high, the feeling of going back to it that night, or I could remember Rayelle and leap right to the consequences.

I was sure I could go home to my recovery house like normal and go to sleep like it never happened and if anyone was still awake in my building, I could easily fool them by acting sober. Which is just ridiculous. And, of course, not at all how it went.

My roommates were awake. They knew right away. I thought about denying it and then I was just so tired. I didn't have it in me to do all of the heartfelt lying I'd need to do when I knew it wouldn't work anyway. Justus was called and I was put in a vacant apartment for the night to sleep it off. The next morning, I woke up and packed up everything I owned.

ᴋ

When we didn't listen, it was usually because we still thought we knew better and could do it alone. Even though some part of us always knew that's how we ended up in all of our messes—not listening, going it alone. People like Justus lectured us anyway, as if the listening didn't matter and the words had to be said no matter what.

Justus arrived to give me and my bags a ride to a sister recovery house. He was a grandfather with perfect posture, expensive-looking jewelry, and clothes that were always pressed carefully, even jeans and T-shirts. Because it was my first offense, he was orchestrating my relocation.

"What you need to do is stop messing with that stuff. You got all these advantages and all these chances. But I see I need to talk to you like you don't know it," he said. "You keep the roof over your head as your top priority. Because that's where you keep your shit. Don't bring anything home that might jeopardize that. Everything valuable is under that roof. That's the place where you can lock out what you need to stay away from. Now I'm taking you somewhere new and you have to start over and have this big disruption in your life. That makes no sense, right?"

Clutching a duffel bag to my chest, I stared out the window and nodded whenever Justus paused his lecture and waited for me to acknowledge him. The day was overcast and a little cool. The heat in Justus's car made me sweat, and I felt so unworthy of the ride, of Justus's time and effort, that I could not bring myself to ask him to turn it down or to even reach out to gently reposition the vent that blew hot air relentlessly into my face.

If you'd asked me then, I would have told you I wasn't going to make it. I wouldn't be in the three-out-of-ten lucky group.

But what I am left with now when I remember that time and that place is the unlikely earnestness of that group of people, of every one of us living together in that building. We were like children, willing to invest our energy into what we knew made no sense, refusing to give up on the impossible. I think of the shame and the regret and the daily cacophony of inner voices screaming at their hosts. We all went there trying to take a step in the right direction for once and most of us probably left that building knowing we'd failed, knowing we'd have to begin again, under any roof that would have us. And in the meantime, we lived with our past and future trying to shake hands because our present was so unbearable and this was what we had in common, this was what we all knew, and even though we fought sometimes, we all made a silent vow to witness this in each other with a sacredness we'd never once summoned in our addictions and never would summon again. We shared our limbo, our fears, but mostly our dingy and threadbare hope. Because it was hope, it shimmered and glowed and swirled in its iridescence all the same. I see you, we said, out there in the courtyard. I'm rooting for you.

Men Raising Their Voices

THE ONE WHO LIVED DOWN THE STREET FROM THE FIRST HOUSE you called home, in a neighborhood of tiny ranch houses and cars on cinder blocks and aboveground pools with torn liners and dogs in pens howling all day. He had a little girl your age that you liked to play with but only if she came outside. Sometimes you could hear him yelling from your own yard and you'd be careful to ride your bike in the other direction for the afternoon.

The one who taught middle school gym, always wearing his red windbreaker and shorts, and screamed at you in the fields, screamed at all the girls like you who couldn't catch balls, run the mile, do a cartwheel. You felt guilty for being so happy when you had an asthma attack and had to walk to the nurse, each precious breath whistling into your lungs, making your chest hurt just to gasp it into your body.

The one who lived right next door, who you never heard yelling, but whose daughter showed up at school at the end of senior year with a black eye, claiming he was the one who gave it to her, and all you could think was, *Yeah, I can see that being true.*

⚬

On my flight home from a friend's book launch event in Austin, Texas, a drunk man yelled. It was my last connecting flight back to

Hartford, Connecticut, a night flight, and I was tired and anxious to see my husband and son.

"What the fuck?" I heard from somewhere behind me, before we'd even left the gate.

I had just opened my book, my carry-on bag already stored in the overhead bin, so I tried to ignore it.

"Well, someone took *my* seat first, for fuck sake," I heard.

We all heard. The man was loud. Sloppy with his volume.

Another man took the seat next to me. We had the row behind first class. Extra leg room.

"Twenty-five dollars to upgrade to this," my seatmate said. I couldn't tell if he was complaining or bragging.

Please stop talking to me, I thought, barely nodding or looking at him so as not to encourage him.

"Do you live in Hartford?" he asked.

"New Haven," I said.

"I'm coming back from a business trip," he said.

"That's nice."

I pulled my book closer to my face.

The yelling behind us started again and when it seemed to be moving up the aisle toward us, I turned to try to get a look.

"All I'm saying is that you better make this right," the man yelled. "I don't give a fuck where you seat me at this point."

The man next to me scrolled through his iPad. I turned back to my book.

Our row shook as the yeller suddenly plopped into the aisle seat on the other side of the businessman.

"Fuck, yeah, an upgrade," he said.

He turned to the businessman and put his fist out.

"Bruh," he said, his eyes half-closed.

The businessman reluctantly fist-bumped him. I smelled the alcohol. I looked at my row partner, sandwiched between the two of us, and he rolled his eyes.

"Hey, hey, hey, stewardess," the drunk yelled. "Get me a drink."

The flight was going to be just under two hours. The pilot came over the speaker, asking us to settle in so we could push off from the gate and be on our way.

"Stewardess!"

I rubbed my face with my hands. It was a full flight. There was nowhere to move, no extra seats.

"I need assistance!" the man said. "What the fuck is up with this seat belt?"

The stewardess came back and leaned forward to look into the man's lap. I held my breath.

"Sir, just pull the side out from beneath you," she said. "It seems you are sitting on the buckle."

"Is this a fucking upgrade?" he answered, tugging at the belt. "Because I need you to get me a drink."

The stewardess just walked away.

"I wouldn't push it," the businessman said to the drunk guy.

"Oh, I'm going to push it," he said.

"Get me a drink!" he screamed.

The plane started to back up while he was still screaming.

A different stewardess came over this time, an older woman. She bent forward so she was at his level, the way a first-grade teacher might for a six-year-old who was misbehaving.

"You need to stop yelling," she said. "You're scaring the other passengers. One more outburst and the pilot is going to take us back to the gate, where we will open the door and let you off. So please. Behave."

Soon we were in the air.

🙠

The one who was the best friend of your boyfriend in high school, who spit beer in your face at a party and screamed, *Cunt*, as loud as he could at you until you were sure the whole town heard, and when your boyfriend left with you, the two of you heard him laughing as you walked to the car, you drying off your face with the edge of your T-shirt, not sure what was beer and what were your tears, and when you looked at your boyfriend walking next to you, you swore you could see a little smirk on his face.

The one who smashed a full-length mirror in your first studio apartment in college, the little place on Lake Shore Drive that you loved so much. He punched the glass out of jealousy and then you had to call your parents and the landlord so you could replace it and not lose your security deposit when the lease ended.

The one you lived with when you were twenty who spit on you and used all his drunken strength to try to hurl you down the stairs while you held on to the banister, saving yourself from serious injury and instead escaping with only a cut on your foot and some bruises. The one who then came in a uniform with a siren, his flashlight illuminating the blood on the stairs, speaking to your boyfriend, saying things like, *Women, what can you do, brother* . . .

🙠

My ex-husband takes me back to court again and again, even though he never seems to get what he wants. He yells in conference rooms and courtrooms, in front of judges and case managers, and still nothing happens. He owes me thousands of dollars in back child support, and each time, the judge asks him if he understands he can be incarcerated for nonpayment, but he still doesn't pay or pays only a small portion of the back support before stopping again. In the fall of 2018, I finally follow my lawyer's advice and open a case with the state enforcement agency because I am all out of chances to give.

I start to sleep with a baseball bat my husband brought up from our basement after my lawyer and I are escorted out of the building by three marshals at their suggestion because of the way my ex-husband behaves in court. This is not the first time the marshals get involved. For every court date in this last round of court dates, the marshals stepped in. They warn him in court when he gets loud, threaten him with jail, and escort me out to prevent any kind of confrontation between us. But my ex-husband moves freely as if he had been polite and reasonable the entire time. His wife walks right up to me even though I feel she emotionally abused my son and the judge said she wasn't supposed to see him or be involved in any of this.

I saw a therapist last year who said she believed I had PTSD from eight years of this. I think it was the pistachio incident when Atlas was five that cemented her diagnosis, the story about the time my son's stepmother fed him nuts right before pickup without telling me, trying to prove I was wrong about allergies, even though I sent paperwork from the pediatric allergist. Atlas broke out in hives by the time we got home and then projectile-vomited in my kitchen.

The next day, I emailed them to report his symptoms and ask them not to give him nuts, per the allergist's order. They immediately called and asked to speak to Atlas. On speakerphone, they instructed him to repeat back to them what they insisted had really happened—he'd just had a "random puke." Atlas hung up the phone and said, "I knew they wouldn't believe me."

This was still not enough to alter the parenting agreement, mostly because I already had primary custody and they did not even have overnights.

But finally, finally, there is no court-ordered visitation and our lives feel safer. My ex-husband has seen my son twice in the last three years with the child psychologist and without the step-mother present, mostly because my child longs to have his dad in his life.

↞

The one who hit his dog because he was mad at you.

The one who ripped a kitchen cabinet door off its hinges in front of the baby and more than once drove out of the driveway screeching his tires and acting so reckless that you were sure every neighbor up and down the street was already at their window. This is the same one who punched things so hard he broke his own hand and then wanted nothing but sympathy for himself.

↞

When people ask me why I was an addict, my best answer is that I was afraid to feel. I grew up being taught that my negative feelings were unacceptable and I should smile more. Like a lot of women, I was afraid to get angry. I stuffed everything. The magic of controlling how I felt all the time with a substance, keeping the doom and the fear and the anger at bay, was just too good to resist. When I am upset or angry now that I am sober, I have to talk myself off the ledge.

It's okay, you won't always feel this way. Just sit with it. It's okay to cry. It's fine to feel rage. It will pass.

When my son was little, I would say, "Do you just need to have a good cry about it? It's okay to cry."

When my plane landed in Hartford, the drunk guy woke up and immediately said, "How the fuck can a person get a goddamn beer around here?" I gathered my things as we taxied to the gate and I watched the baggage handlers on the tarmac as they lined up the cart, ready to unload our suitcases. They looked cold. It was late and dark. The drunk guy rambled on and no one stopped him. No one asked him to keep his voice down, to stop yelling. We all just waited until we could get away from him.

❦

The ones you know you are forgetting now, no matter how carefully you flip backward through your memories, go over them looking for rage.

The one you are raising who is only twelve, who you think might never be on any woman's list years from now, because you have always said, since he was very small, *It's okay to be sad and cry. Come and have a long cry next to me. I'll stay with you so you don't cry alone. Everybody cries sometimes.*

❦

Walking through the almost-empty airport, I wanted to get home to hug my son. I knew on the counter there would be a pile of mail for me. My husband had already warned me that there was a letter from the state child support enforcement agency waiting for me. Probably the documentation of the last court date when my ex-husband's motion for a support modification had been denied.

As I followed the signs to ground transportation, I saw the drunk man from my flight. He'd found two women to walk with and, calmer now, he related his flight experience, making himself out to be the victim, using them to process the conflict. As I passed the three of them, I glanced over quickly, curious to see the faces of the women. Their body language told me they wanted him to move on.

Like radar, he seemed to sense my presence immediately and leaned forward to see me on the other side of his new reluctant companions. I wore my blank face, my no-emotion face, prepared just in case the drunk guy's gaze happened to settle on me, like a landing place for all his grievances.

Turnpike

THIS IS THE STORY, THE MEMORY, AND THESE ARE THE IMAGES that come back to me when I think of the hardest years after the divorce, when Atlas was four or five.

I am the custodial parent and my ex-husband has short visits. He remarries the day after the judge grants our divorce. His new house with his new wife is about twenty minutes from the marital home where Atlas and I remain.

This is the road I take twice a week to pick up my boy. These are the traffic lights I stop for or rush through, depending on the minutes glowing at me from my dashboard clock. That's the dinosaur miniature golf course built into the side of the hill next to the bowling alley. There are too many gas stations to count dotting the side of this four-lane stretch of highway. It isn't the neon logos of chain stores that catch my eye each time. It's the strange collection of little motels that stun me with their determination to stay in business. This is the turnpike I take for twelve miles on Tuesday and Thursday nights when I bring my child home from his court-ordered visitation.

I pass a strip club and stare as I drive by. The parking lot is never empty. The lights are always on. Sometimes a girl stands outside next to the bouncer, smoking a cigarette. I slow down to see her better because there is something I want to know about the girls who work there.

When I think the stepmother, let's call her Dina, is being awful to my son, I have the craziest thoughts. She cut off his hair, claiming he looked like a girl. I believe she may even play a game when she steps in front of automatic doors with my child, saying to him, *Open the gate, who do you hate, I hate Cindy*. She throws away a T-shirt and rain boots, Atlas's favorites, both with skull images from the Gap Kids pirate line that year, saying she doesn't allow "death skulls" in her house. In front of Atlas, she photographs the inside of his tiny backpack, from the same Gap Kids line that year, because there's a skull on the label. Sometimes I imagine how it would feel to take a match and hold it to the hem of her skirt or at the bottom of her thick, bristly, ridiculous hair. I can see myself removing one shoe and using the heel to gouge holes in her miserable face. I hate the way her smile turns downward, the way it makes her skin look as if it is melting. I remember being five, and at that age, Dina would have been the truest version of a witch that I could've imagined.

Other nights, I have visions with less violence, less mess. I daydream about stopping at Centerfold's and introducing myself to the girls who dance there. I imagine hiring one of them to show up at my ex-husband's door in a thin strappy dress armed with personal details and a screechy claim of pregnancy.

I see myself in a tan trench coat handing a young dancer in a thong a photo of Dina.

Make sure the stepmother is with him before you start, I imagine myself saying. *Here's a photo of her.*

I never do that. I always decide not to do that. It seems to me that hiring third-party strangers never works out. The news is full of people coming forward to say they'd been hired to kill, kidnap, lie.

After she sends me an email I view as completely unhinged, ten pages of exclamation points and claims that I don't feed or clothe my child properly, that I don't care about his life, I start dressing up for pickup. I read the lines demanding that all discussion about my son go through her from now on and I know it's adolescent but there I am, strutting down their cracked tar driveway in high heels, blown-out hair, full makeup, and a little black dress. The old me might have thought it was a little obvious, a little transparent, but the new me, the me dealing with the stepmother, knows that obvious is the only way to go.

Those times when I feel her eyes traveling up and down my body, the one night when I watch her stomp back into their house and slam the door, it's like winning, and when I hug my boy and carry him to my car, it feels good to know who is angry and afraid now. But by the time I get home, I'm horrified by who I am becoming.

My lawyer is sympathetic; he answers my texts, calls, emails, immediately. I document everything and wait. I think strategically. I bite my tongue. I comfort Atlas. I find a pediatric allergist, a naturopath, a child psychologist.

I am afraid of everything. I hide my son's passport and worry they will find a way to take him. I fear things I can't even let myself think about.

This isn't what I imagined when I thought of becoming someone's mother.

One night, I stop at the last light before I leave the turnpike and something makes me look to the side of the road. It's a small pair of eyes glinting in the pale melon-colored streetlight. Animals have become so aggressive, I think. Or maybe I heard that somewhere. Who said that?

Possum, I think as the light turns green and I step on the gas. I saw a possum in broad daylight the week before at Atlas's school. That's where I'd heard the phrase about aggression. Another mother said that to me as the two of us watched the possum walk toward the children near the sandbox. The animal's white fur had looked stained and oily and I'd noticed it swaying, leaning toward one side and then the other.

"Maybe it's high," I'd said, grinning. But she never laughed or even smiled. Instead, she stared at me.

"We should tell someone," she'd said. "Don't you think we should tell someone?"

She thought the animal might be dangerous.

"A possum out in the daytime, it's got to be sick," she said.

After I take the right off the turnpike, I coast down the hill, past the handful of houses before my ex's. I swerve into his driveway and my eyes land on the window where I always look for my son's little head behind the glass. The house is completely dark, not a single light anywhere, but their cars are in the driveway.

They've finally done something, I think.

My best friend at age thirteen, Sandy, had a regular babysitting job with this one family on her block. I used to go with her often. Sandy and I would ignore the baby and nervously dial boys we liked, praying their mothers wouldn't answer. There were no cell phones then, we were just kids.

The family had one baby at that time, a boy named Robbie. I never remember the baby crying. When I think of him now, I can still see his big dark eyes and his inky straight hair and his surprised expression.

Back then, people used playpens for babies. Sandy used to plop the baby into it and sometimes the two of us would leave the room for a very long time to pick at things in their refrigerator or look through their drawers or talk on the phone, twirling the long cord around our wrists. I never once questioned the baby's silence or even talked about how strange it was that he never cried.

Sandy and I stopped being friends the following year. She told me the boy I liked couldn't stand me, said I was fat. I told her that I thought she had a weak chin and her profile was ugly, something my mother had pointed out to me after the first time she met Sandy.

I never missed her.

Then one day in my senior year of high school, I picked up part of the newspaper from the kitchen table where my dad had left it and saw this family's name in the headline.

The parents had had one more child and then a nasty separation. Divorce negotiations had been difficult, the paper said.

The article was about the dad shooting Robbie and his younger sister in the head as they sat in the back of his car, supposedly on their way to Six Flags Amusement Park, which is what the father told their mother. One, two, and then a bullet for himself, the rifle held between his knees when they were all found in the car.

And so that night, in my ex-husband's driveway in front of

his dark house, I picture little Robbie as my shaking hands dig for my cell phone in my purse. Picture his face as I push the right numbers, swallowing again and again to stay calm, my eyes on the large picture window where I usually saw my little son's head.

It rings and it rings and it rings. With each ring, I hear myself whisper, "Please, please, please."

What a stupid, stupid girl I have always been, I think.

And then I hear Atlas's little voice, like a hallucination, until his body is suddenly in front of my headlights, my ex and Dina closing in behind him. They are coming from a visit to their neighbor's house.

I stumble out of my car, my legs wobbly. I pick up my son and wordlessly carry him to the back door, strap him into his car seat.

This is the memory I relive, the road I drive again and again, the thoughts that return, the thumping of my pulse, the shaking of my hands.

In the more than three years since my son has had no visitation with his father and Dina, his anecdotes and memories have confirmed my suspicion that visits were worse than I knew. The time they made him spend the entire visit, hours, sitting alone at their table, refusing something he could not eat, sobbing and not knowing when it would end. The time his stepmother printed out fake documents and told him he would be living with them instead of me. The time they made him say he wasn't really allergic to dogs. The time Dina said that she was tired of my five-year-old treating her like shit.

For years, I'd assumed that my addiction was the worst thing that would ever happen to me, but that was before I had a child who was vulnerable to things I could not control.

Part of me is still sitting in my car in the dark in their driveway, my heart in my throat, panicked, terrified. Part of my son is still crying at their table, waiting for me to pick him up and take him home.

Comfort in Stories

IN 1990, WHEN I WAS TWENTY-THREE AND MANY YEARS AWAY from motherhood, I left college for my home state, where I spent one long winter at the Yale Psychiatric Institute in New Haven, Connecticut. When I checked in, suffering from severe clinical depression, I had just cut my hair off and hadn't slept more than a couple of hours a night for months.

I remember the sound of the scissors, the way it felt to try to close the blades over my thick ponytail. It wasn't the fast satisfying snip I'd imagined when I couldn't sleep at night in my loft space in Chicago, the roof leaking a heartbeat of drips that echoed in the huge, empty space. I had to divide the ponytail into sections and then force the blades slowly through each one until my hand cramped.

The hospital stay felt much the same way. Instead of a quick cure as soon as I'd made the awful decision to sign myself in, I languished for weeks, still feeling too depressed to recognize myself or anything I'd ever loved. The doctors wanted to question me about sleeping and eating, but what I really needed them to know was that I found myself unable to read. From the time I first learned how to read, I always carried a book. Books were my company, my counsel, my escape from every uncomfortable feeling. In my depression, I could latch on to a word here and there, but whole paragraphs were indecipherable. They asked me repeatedly about suicidal ideation, but I kept thinking, *Don't you understand? I can no longer read.*

The meds took time to work, so instead of lying awake all night in my own bed where I could chain-smoke and watch reruns of *America's Most Wanted*, I had to lie awake in my tiny twin hospital bed with a snoring roommate on the other side of the room and nurses doing fifteen-minute bed checks throughout the night.

When spring finally pushed winter aside, when my meds were stabilized and I was sleeping again after weeks of inpatient treatment, I decided I was as good as I was going to get and I might as well say the things that would secure a discharge date. I was sent home with the prescriptions that would guarantee sleep, and I went back to my life in Chicago, renting a new basement apartment that felt like a cave. It's difficult to measure wellness when it comes to mental health, especially from the inside of a long clinical depression, but I knew I still wasn't myself.

It was summer by then, and I spent time in bookstores for the air-conditioned ways to get lost. I was just starting to read again, the surest sign of hope for recovery that anyone could offer me. One day I decided, out of nowhere, to read everything I could about the Vietnam War. I started with nonfiction. When that didn't satisfy the need I couldn't define, I asked a bookstore employee to recommend stories about the war. This was how I discovered Tim O'Brien, specifically his book *The Things They Carried*.

I have no doubt that the book is the thing that cured me, that pushed me out of depression. It wasn't sleeping again or the antidepressants; it was a collection of short stories. I can't hear the title or Tim O'Brien's name without seeing myself in bed, curled into the fetal position with that book in front of my face.

Alone in my basement apartment, I started to imagine feeling joy again: "Because it's all relative. You're pinned down in some filthy hellhole of a paddy, getting your ass delivered to kingdom come, but then for a few seconds everything goes quiet and you look up and see the sun and a few puffy white clouds, and the immense serenity flashes against your eyeballs—the whole world gets rearranged—and even though you're pinned down by a war you never felt more at peace." The words made me envision my own survival. I know how this sounds, and I certainly never talked about it with anyone back then. I was a privileged college girl from Connecticut who had no idea where the depression came from, and Tim O'Brien was talking about watching friends get blown up and seeing the very worst that this world has to show. But somehow, it saved me. I needed to fall into something worse than my own reality. I needed perspective. I needed to understand that humans had survived far worse than depression and had even gone on to write about it.

Tim O'Brien's book made me feel less alone.

In a scene where O'Brien sits in a boat on a river between the United States and Canada, trying to force himself to run away, to evade the war, he writes: "Everywhere, it seemed, in the trees and water and sky, a great worldwide sadness came pressing down on me, a crushing sorrow, sorrow like I had never known it before."

By the time I reached the end of the book, I'd started spending less time in bed, and I'd even begun to apply for waitressing jobs. I'd started to think about finishing my degree at the School of the Art Institute of Chicago. It was as if a debilitating fever had flattened me for the better part of a year and now I was finally well, standing up and looking in the fridge, feeling hungry for the first time in months.

And I thought about writing again. The final piece in *The Things They Carried* opens with the line, "But this too is true: stories can save us." Not only had I been saved, but like a born-again, newly devoted follower, I wanted to write stories that would save others. I wanted to worship at the house of words and study the wisdom of those who had come before me. I was ready to join the living and persevere.

This is what a book did for me all those years ago.

ᴋ

When I found myself feeling helpless as a mother more than twenty years later, when Atlas seemed to be falling apart as a response to my divorce, his father's immediate remarriage to someone who I thought treated him poorly, and the complicated coparenting relationship that resulted, I thought about new books for Atlas.

One specific day in Atlas's first year of school stands out when I think about his suffering. He was attending a co-op that one of the parents liked to call "the little hippie school." There were only eight kids, and we parents pooled our money to rent the space where school was held and to pay the wonderful teacher who spent those days with our children. Things had been getting worse and worse for Atlas; he was more and more out of control, crying, screaming, accusing the other kids of leaving him out or picking on him. It was winter, and after school the kids would all play in the yard for a while as the parents stood around chatting. I didn't see what sparked it, but Atlas was suddenly screaming at the other kids, who mostly stared at him openmouthed, or turned their backs on his noise to continue the game they were playing. I went to him and tried to get him to talk to me, tried to get him to walk away so he could calm down. He wouldn't budge. I myself was frozen, ineffective and scared—and embarrassed, if I'm honest. Everyone could see that I could not reach my own child.

I abruptly went down in front of my screaming son, knees in the snow, and put my hands up.

"Show me how angry you are," I said, looking into his face. "Push against my hands as hard as you can and show me how angry you are."

My knees were already becoming numb inside my soaking-wet jeans. My son leaned into my hands, pushing with all his weight and grunting and growling with rage. It felt like a victory just to have him follow my directions.

"I see you," I said. "I see how angry you are. My, you are so angry right now."

His rage dissipated and melted into sobs. Heartbreaking, gut-wrenching sobs. I felt humbled, drained, shocked, terrified. *Maybe he would never be okay*, I thought.

I had begun to read chapter books to Atlas like *The Mouse and the Motorcycle*, *Charlotte's Web*, and *Frog and Toad*, but he needed stories that could be true, real characters he could relate to, fictional kids who had struggles as big as or bigger than his own. He understood that his friends at school weren't acting the way he was, but it's hard to explain to a five-year-old that his friends weren't living the same trauma.

I took him home on a weepy afternoon that winter, and we got in bed, and I cracked open the book *Wonder* by R. J. Palacio, a novel about a boy who was born with a severe facial deformity and has to navigate school for the first time after being homeschooled all his life because of extensive medical treatment.

The main character, August, discovers that kids can be unkind when he overhears them saying awful things about the way he looks: "And I started crying. I couldn't keep it from happening. The tears were so thick in my eyes I could barely see, but I couldn't wipe them through the mask as I walked. I was looking for a little tiny spot to disappear into. I wanted a hole I could fall inside of: a little black hole that would eat me up."

I looked at my sad son and saw that he was glued to my voice, listening with every part of his being.

One day, more than halfway through the book, we read, "I ran down the hallway to my room and slammed the door behind me so hard that I actually heard little pieces of the wall crumble inside the door frame." Atlas looked at me and said, "I've been that mad before." He could say it out loud because he knew he wasn't the only kid who had felt that kind of rage.

Storytelling became the same light in the dark for Atlas that it is for me, the path to find our way, the hand held out to us so we're not alone. *Wonder* taught my son that we each carry these struggles and we don't have to bury them and let them fester. They are fine living right up near the surface. A book is possibility, what we are capable of enduring, shared emotion and struggle that runs like a thread of meaning through our lives.

In the last few years, Atlas has been in indie films where he has played an abused foster kid, a lonely boy spying on teenagers, a bully, a neighborhood kid in the Bronx who witnesses an assault, and the stoic child of an eccentric man who remains closed off to him. Each time, he slips into the skin of someone new. At first I wondered how he knew how to act. He landed roles immediately. Then I realized acting is believing the reality of a character's existence, falling into the story because you keep your own struggles close at hand and not buried in the dark. When the camera stops, when the book closes, we come back to our own life, better for the experience of living someone else's for a little while.

Morton's Fork

IN THE FIRST DAYS OF 2015, I FOUND A SONG THAT FELT WRITTEN for me.

It was right after a six-month reprieve for Atlas and me from the divorce chaos. My ex-husband had decided to separate from his wife and Atlas stopped seeing her for those months. Without the stepmother, I got along with my ex. Within two weeks of not having to see her, Atlas was like a new child. The emotional outbursts stopped, the anxiety dissipated, he laughed and smiled more, slept better, and articulated his joy that he was free of her.

I no longer received what I considered petty emails from the stepmother. I could count on my ex to pick up or drop off on time and Atlas didn't come home and cry anymore. We went on this way all summer and through the fall, over Christmas, into the new year, and I allowed myself to believe my ex-husband when he said he was divorcing her. When he told me he thought she was abusive to Atlas and he was done, I took him at his word.

I had just been accepted into my MFA program at Lesley University and I had just started to date my second husband when my ex announced he was reuniting with his wife.

I kept thinking about how the clinic where I'd brought Atlas for therapy had told me he had been redlined for a depression diagnosis before the separation. I thought about the stress he'd been under, the petty things, in my opinion, she did to him, the multiple melt-downs a day that he'd had when she was in his life. I did not know how we could possibly go back. I spent days not sleeping or eating, making phone calls to my lawyer and to Atlas's psychology team. No one had the answer I needed—assurance that Atlas wouldn't have to see her again.

The song begins with a dramatic sweep of three horns and two violins, rising in volume. Then the horns drop off and softer notes are plucked on a ukulele accompanied by a steel brush scratching rhythmically across a drum. Then the guitar comes in, melodic, holding back. I want to move closer to hear better. The lead singer leans into the mic and sings, "I told you, Ma, I'll keep you safe."

The song is "Morton's Fork" by Typhoon, an eleven-member band from Portland, Oregon. They weren't new in 2015; they were just new to me. I heard their song "Young Fathers" one night on NPR and bought the CD *White Lighter*, which included "Morton's Fork."

Psychology Wiki defines Morton's Fork as "an expression that describes a choice between two equally unpleasant alternatives (in other words, a dilemma), or two lines of reasoning that lead to the same unpleasant conclusion. It is analogous to the expressions '*between the devil and the deep blue sea*' or '*between a rock and a hard place.*'"

Between the fall of 2011, when Atlas was four, and the summer of 2017, when he was almost ten, I had lived with one constant Morton's Fork scenario: If I sent Atlas to his court-ordered visitation, minimal though it was, he would be emotionally damaged. If I did not honor the visitation and instead kept him home, I would risk losing custody for being in contempt.

In family court, there is never really a moment where you get to sit down and tell your story, express your concerns. If it is not provable serious abuse, there are not many options. I tried to reason with my ex-husband and his wife. I tried being nice. Once, I even brought a bag of groceries over filled with alternatives to the foods listed on Atlas's testing paperwork as allergens. This resulted in rage, with the stepmother coming out to the driveway at my five p.m. pickup in her robe and slippers, yelling at me, "Do you have a problem with me?" I did. I had a lot of problems with her.

It didn't matter to the family court judge that Atlas completely melted down before every visit, refused to go, begged to stay home. It didn't matter that they fed him things he was allergic to and ignored his severe dog allergy. It didn't matter that my ex-husband owed thousands in child support arrears.

꙳

After my ex and his wife got back together, it kept snowing. Storm after storm dumped inches on us. Atlas and I were living in a building in downtown Middletown, Connecticut, where we were friendly with our neighbors. There was a tiny parking lot behind the building for our cars, and every time it snowed we shoveled as a group, all the tenants from the four apartments in the building.

One of our neighbors was a fifth-grade teacher who gave us a homemade blueberry pie when we moved in and who climbed on the eave over the front door in costume to hand out candy in a lowered bucket on Halloween. When it snowed, he always had a shovel for Atlas and jokes to make him laugh.

I think of us bundling up in the dark winter evening and going out to meet our neighbors, me trying not to cry over the kindness shown to Atlas, feeling grateful he was laughing in that moment. I wanted to tell these neighbors I barely knew how sick and sad I was, how I had no solution to this horrible situation in our life.

The snowstorms gave me a little time because the roads were too bad to drive him for visitation. At night, after Atlas fell asleep, I would walk around the apartment, looking out at the snow, crying, trying to think of any way I might save my son.

☞

Kyle Morton, the lead singer in Typhoon, has said in interviews that many of his songs are about his childhood battle with near-fatal Lyme disease. He writes about how to love is to risk, to be vulnerable; and no matter what you do to protect your loved ones, we all die in the end.

Shortly into the first verse, after Morton sings, "I thought we'd live forever, a simple obstacle in the way," the backup singers sing, "Let it go, let it go, let it go." At the time when I'd first found the song and listened to it constantly, those three *let it go*'s would almost break me. Because, of course, there was nothing about what was happening that I could ever let go.

☞

When Atlas found out that his father would not be getting a divorce after all, he became hysterical. He screamed he would not go back. Cried and yelled, "Why?" He was only seven and a half. He had gotten used to peace. He was getting to know his dad again with one-on-one time.

After the first visitation after his stepmother's return, Atlas came home to tell me that his stepmother was getting a Porsche and that she and his father would be tattooing each other's names on their bodies. It reminded me of an earlier time when he came home and asked me, "Mom, what are uterine fibroids?" Apparently the stepmother had used visitation to discuss her uterus with my five-year-old and how God might give her a baby. She was fifty-one at the time, so God might have needed a fertility doctor, but none of that was information my child needed to hear.

When my ex-husband asked me if I'd go to therapy with them, I said yes. I figured at the very least it would be like a reconnaissance mission where I could learn more about what Atlas was dealing with. They picked a Christian family therapist who saw patients in his home.

☙

I'd been taking Atlas to therapy at the University of Connecticut, where they saw kids on a sliding scale. It was an hour each way but it was what I could afford and it was helpful for him. On the drive I'd put in the Typhoon CD and try not to cry through "Morton's Fork."

The place where the song really feels eerily like my own thoughts is when Kyle Morton sings, "It turns out that we are shit out of luck. There are things in the woods that will prey on the things that you love."

I'd felt like we'd been preyed upon for years by then. She cut my child's hair off without asking and against his will. When I still lived in the marital house, I think she told Atlas that our house was hers and she was going to take it, she was going to make us get out, even though the divorce agreement stipulated our residence in said house. It seems that she also told Atlas there were bugs in the beds in my house and then showed him videos about bedbugs. For weeks I had to peel back the fitted sheets on our beds to show him there were no bugs. He had nightmares about insects for months.

In the very first therapy session with them, the therapist was talking about respect, and when the stepmother insisted on looking up the definition on her phone, the therapist said, "Please don't do that." And she started to cry. And then she wouldn't speak. When the therapist asked her about it, she denied being upset.

At the next therapy session, the stepmother came barefoot and walked across the therapist's dewy grass so when she reached the front door, her feet were filthy and she came inside like that. My ex slammed his stainless-steel water bottle down on the therapist's glass coffee table within minutes and stormed out. The stepmother brought a folder with papers, and from what I could see they included a printout of a puppy Atlas thought was cute (I guess to prove that he didn't have a dog allergy?), and a paper diner place mat where he had colored a picture of the three of them. In this session of therapy between me and the stepmother, she lay down on the therapist's couch and used her pink fleece jacket as a blanket and said, "I'm listening," with her eyes closed.

For the third and final session, the stepmother got lost on the way there and my ex-husband had to leave and find where she was and then lead her to the therapist's house. I think she tried to drive separately so I could see her Porsche, but I'm only guessing. Again, my ex stormed out and I was left with the stepmother.

There was one point in that session where she said, "I could tell him all about your past." I'm not sure the therapist heard her and he moved on to something else, but I wish I had replied. I don't know exactly what I would have said, but I'm still disappointed in myself. I'm also surprised she hadn't tried to use it against me before that moment. For years, I told myself either my ex-husband wasn't listening the one time I mentioned my past to him or he completely forgot about it. But to hear her try to threaten me with that was chilling. I stared at her from my armchair and understood everything I needed to know about why Atlas cried every time he had to see her.

And then the therapist agreed with me one time too many and they fired him.

ϰ

Right after I found out Atlas's dad and stepmother were getting back together, I took a friend and her son out to lunch to thank them for taking Atlas one day a couple of months earlier so I could finish my grad school applications. It was a fancy Mexican restaurant in West Hartford, with white tablecloths and guacamole made table-side and a glass shelf all along the back of the bar filled with top-shelf tequila. It was a weekday and packed with people in suits. I felt lost and bereft. Atlas and I waited by the bar for our friends and I stared at the glasses and the bottles and then at the people on barstools, smiling and clinking their martini glasses. As if it were a solid, concrete object being born, my longing formed and intensified. It wasn't so much a craving for the feeling of being high or drunk; it was a yearning for the option to escape for just a little while, to have a break, to change the inescapable problem I was staring at night and day. Atlas leaned against me and I reached down and touched his hair, my eyes welling up with guilt for even just wishing for that kind of relief. He didn't know it, but he needed me more than ever and I was ashamed for being hypnotized by the sound of a cocktail shaker.

🖝

"Morton's Fork" builds in the middle and several people in the band join in to sing, "We are alone in this together, all alone in this together, all alone." And then the group starts to sing in a howl, a howl like a pack of wolves, together with the ascendant horns into a cacophony of what I heard as sorrowful desperation. If I made a sound to express what it felt like to send my son off to visitation, what would have come out of my mouth would have been that howling.

The howling, the horns, the drums, all of it comes to a stop and then there is just one soft guitar and Morton sings, "I haven't slept in several nights and I'm not tired. Who protects the ones I love when I'm asleep? Though there's little I can do, I say a prayer that when the wolves come for their share, they'll come for me." That final line felt like my wish that the suffering would only be on me, that I could take the brunt of whatever they had to dish out and leave Atlas out of it. *Come for me, not Atlas*, I wanted to say. Morton's voice cracks on those lines, the way mine would, had I been forced to sing them back in early 2015.

Not every crisis comes with a soundtrack, a theme song perfectly written for you, and even under my desperate anxiety and gloom, I knew to be grateful for that song. There was something about Kyle Morton's intensity that soothed me, served as a balm.

Someone out there, a person I could watch on my computer, was feeling things deeply, and it hurt him. And he was making something beautiful with that. We were both mourning someone's childhood and it made me feel less alone.

About two years after the reunion of my ex and his wife, Atlas's new psychologist felt the need to call the Connecticut Department of Child Protection. My ex-husband dropped all contact for nine months and then brought me back to court to try to lower the child support he hadn't been paying. He lost. By the time we were back in court, Atlas was eleven and my lawyer asked for a family case manager to interview him so he could say that he didn't want to see his stepmother again. The judge listened. Atlas has not seen her or heard from her in three and a half years as of this writing. The door is open for his father to see him alone at some point, and that may happen. But the stepmother is not welcome.

In 2018, my husband Gian-Carl surprised me with tickets to see Typhoon at a small local venue. Before the show started, I saw Kyle Morton standing by a table with CDs and T-shirts for sale. I thought of going over to talk to him, but I never do that kind of thing. I didn't know how to tell him what that song meant to me.

We stood just a few feet from the stage. They didn't play "Morton's Fork," which was almost a relief. I can still cry when I hear it. I thought about how light and happy Kyle Morton seemed up there. *Of course*, I thought. The things that haunt us can be left behind in what we make, held safe where they won't continue to torture us. Maybe that is what drives us to make art out of the worst things that happen to us. Maybe for some of us, that is how we survive.

I'm Here to See David Sedaris

December 2019

I STAND IN THE WINGS ONSTAGE WITH ATLAS AND DAVID. A radio personality from NPR is at the podium, listing David's books and all of the languages they've been translated into. Atlas is calm, a mic in his hand, ready and waiting for the NPR guy to call him out.

He strides confidently to the spotlight and begins his introduction for David. I can't see much of the audience, can only feel the breath and life and mass of what I know is a large crowd. I am staring at the silhouette of my kid out there, outlined in that yellow glow like a halo. I can't focus on what he's saying, but then I hear the laugh. Another few lines, and another laugh. And then David is walking out to him, shaking his hand, sending him back to me.

"A fearless child," David says to the audience. He introduces me as the mother of the fearless child and I walk to the podium for my turn to read a seven-minute essay as David's opener.

The lights blind me to the crowd and the seven minutes rush by.

Later, Atlas and I listen to the rest of the show in David's dressing room in the basement of the theater, David's voice coming through the speakers loud and clear, filling the room. In an essay about his sister Amy, David talks about the feeling of seeing her perform. He says, "There is no greater pleasure than feeling proud of someone you love."

Without speaking, Atlas and I smile at each other from across the dressing room, and at the same time we both slowly lift our arms and point to each other.

October 2016

At a hotel eight minutes from my home in New Haven, I go up to the reception desk and say, "I'm here to see David Sedaris."

For decades now, I've been meeting him twice a year at the hotels where he stays on his tours. In Marriotts and Ramada Inns, Ritz-Carltons and Four Seasons, I have walked up to front desks to ask for him.

I see him crossing the lobby. I introduce him to my new husband, Gian-Carl. We step out onto the New Haven sidewalk into perfect fall weather. The leaves on the edges of the Yale campus glow yellow and whisper above us.

At a café, we take an outdoor table in the sun. Friends of mine are joining us soon. David asks me how my essay is coming along. This essay.

"It's such a hard thing to write," I say.

A month earlier he had sent me an email offering to never read the essay if it would help me to write it.

When my friends join us, we end up talking about our children. I say that Atlas has been very interested in the Holocaust since he was seven. Without hesitating, my friend Allison nods knowingly and says, "Slavery." Her six-year-old daughter is obsessed with slavery. This conversation makes David cackle.

In the crowded theater that night, I sit next to my husband in the dark, a notebook on my lap so I can email comments to David about his new work when I get home.

The anchor story is about his sister Tiffany, her suicide, their estrangement, and how she struggled most of her adult life with mental illness and substance abuse. I scribble thoughts and admire the huge risk he takes. When he gets to the part where he remembers the last time he saw her alive, I stop writing. He reads about Tiffany showing up at one of his shows unannounced after years of no contact between them. He delivers a line of dialogue in her voice and pauses. I feel the entire audience holding its breath with me, seeing Tiffany's ghost on the stage. And then he reads that he closed the door in her face.

When I email David to tell him how much I loved the piece, he writes that he fears it will make people hate him. I know something about the terrible way addicts treat their loved ones, because I used to be one of those addicts.

I want to offer him some kind of forgiveness. I know that every addiction is different. Each addict is her own galaxy of misery, her own specific mess. But I tell him that people won't hate him because many people have had a Tiffany in their lives. Still others will have been the Tiffany in someone else's life, like me. I tell him that we know we are horrible and we don't hold it against the people who need to close the door in our faces.

August 2016

In my in-box, I find an email from David with the subject line "1989." He has sent me a photo he took of a diary entry from when we first knew each other. It's about how proud he was of me after my first reading. I wonder if he is sending me this because he knows I'm writing about him.

It took a decade of recovery before I emailed David one night to tell him that I thought he saved my life. No matter how hard you try, you can't completely give up on yourself when someone you admire refuses to give up on you first. When I asked David if he'd mind if I wrote about our friendship, he emailed back:

> *Feel free to write about me at any time and to say bad things if you need to. It would not affect our friendship. I'd think, Look what Cindy wrote! The phrasing is so good when she calls me an asshole!*

I stare closely at the photo of his diary entry, at the typeset on the page, and then at the rustic wooden table beneath. I wonder if that is his desk in England.

It would never occur to me to call him an asshole.

April 2016

We drive to the Stamford Marriott where David is staying. My eight-year-old is with me for the first time, anxious to meet the person who has been sending him postcards for years.

When Atlas was six, his therapist, a huge Sedaris fan, didn't believe that they were pen pals. Atlas looked at him grinning and said, "Brett, are you jealous of my postcards?"

The Marriott is enormous and I remember meeting David here one other time a few years earlier. We sat in armchairs surrounded by plants and it was raining. He talked about the shirt he was wearing and how big the buttons were, and just before we parted so he could change before the show ("Don't worry," he said. "I'm not wearing this onstage."), I told him I was getting a divorce.

"I'm here to see David Sedaris," I tell the front desk person.

When he comes into the lobby, we move to the plant-infested bar area. He tells us he thinks this hotel is a dump. I watch Atlas look up at the enormous domed glass ceiling and then down at the little stream and waterfall surrounding the bar and I know what he's thinking. *This guy is nuts—it's the fanciest hotel ever.*

He gives Atlas a box full of presents. Inside there is candy from a medical museum in London, chocolate eyeballs and gummy brains. There are so many presents that Atlas is overwhelmed. A tin from Japan with delicate cookies inside. An owl night-light, a blank journal, a book with beautiful animal drawings that can be shifted and combined into new creatures. I worry that my child doesn't seem grateful. He isn't really thanking David, just eating a ridiculous amount of the candy. Nerves, I know.

Atlas starts to do his impression of Marty, the grouchy old Hollywood agent. His fingers bend to accommodate an imaginary cigar, he starts talking in a raspy voice, and he barks at us convincingly. My mother and I laugh, but David is quiet. I want to tell him, *David's a tough audience, kid. When you think you're being hilarious, he won't even crack a smile. And then when you say something serious, he'll cackle out of nowhere.*

January 2016

At my second residency for my MFA program, I find myself exhausted and upset one night after a full day of seminars. I doubt the new mentor I've been assigned. I madly march my way through Harvard Square back to the Airbnb place I've rented. I email David, discouraged and wanting to cry. He writes back:

> *The things you told yourself—that you may never write again, that you won't have a career—are the things everyone tells him or her self. It's good to feel like that every so often and then to do exactly what you did: stomp home and get to work.*

I am almost embarrassed by my good fortune in having David Sedaris as a support. For thirty years, I've been waiting for someone to tell me I don't deserve this kind of loyalty, waiting to hear that the friendship has been revoked. When I return to campus early the next morning for more seminars and workshops, I tell no one about this email exchange.

October 2015

In Northampton, Massachusetts, I approach the front desk of the hotel. The last time David stayed here, they would not call his room, apparently thinking I might be a deranged stalker. They told me there was no one registered by that name. When I tried to protest, saying I knew he was there because he was a friend of mine and he told me to meet him at this hotel, they told me I should call his cell phone if I was such a good friend. I said he didn't have a cell phone, which made me sound exactly like a stalker. Then I looked across the lobby and saw him sitting in an armchair by the entrance, waiting for me.

"I'm here to see David Sedaris," I say.

This time, the woman manning the counter picks up the phone and says, "Who may I say is here to see him?"

We sit in a Starbucks for an hour or so. I explain the craft annotations I have to write each semester for my MFA, short papers where I look at specific craft elements employed by various writers. He says he doesn't think he could write something like that. Maybe he doesn't remember all the times he's talked about books over the years, why he loved something or why he felt something failed.

I think about this quality of humility in writers. In interviews, all of my favorite writers have it. Once, in a letter of recommendation, David wrote that when I was his student at age nineteen, he worried I could see right through him.

When we make our way to the front door for the walk back to his hotel, the man behind the counter who made our drinks approaches David. His hands shake as he wipes them on his apron. He hesitates. Then he jumps in.

"Mr. Sedaris," he says. "I'm sorry to bother you, but I just wanted to tell you how much your work means to me."

I wander away, pretending to browse the various coffee mugs and single-press coffeepots on the shelves, trying to give the guy some privacy and not listen in to his moment. Finally, David joins me and we step outside.

"When that happens to you, does it ever bother you?"

"Are you kidding me?" David says. "It's all I've ever wanted since I was eight years old."

September 2015

Out of the blue, an acquaintance from college contacts me on Face-book. He has a video from our old performance art class at the School of the Art Institute of Chicago. It's a short clip of all of us at the professor's home on Logan Boulevard.

I don't watch the video right away. I peek in on my sleeping son. It's late and I am working on my first submission of my first semester of my MFA program. My new husband is in Italy with his grown son. The house is quiet. I climb back in bed with my laptop.

I'm writing a craft annotation on narcissism as part of the char-acterization of the protagonist in an Ethan Canin short story.

The video link is from 1988. I am twenty-one. I'm both afraid and curious to open it.

The camera pans through a dark hallway and then into a dining room filled with light. Voices weave in and out, glasses clink, a phone rings. The professor's house is crowded.

I see myself sitting between two other people at the dining room table. I am wearing a buttoned-up white shirt and a David Byrne oversized white suit jacket. I am clinging to a full wineglass in one hand, and in the other I clutch a lit cigarette.

I recognize my own voice immediately and catch a few sen-tences of a story I told a lot back then. It sounds unbearably stupid now. It's about a job I had folding sweaters. How I hated the cus-tomers who came along and lifted up my perfectly folded items, shaking them out of their little square of tidiness, just to hold them up, frown, and drop them in a heap back on the display.

No one sitting near me in the video seems to be listening, and who can blame them?

I watch the video again, and all I can think is that anyone looking at that stiff, rambling girl in white would be able to predict the kind of disaster that culminates in needles or jail or death. I look at that girl with hands hoarding substances. Anyone could predict that this was a person who would fail spectacularly.

It was right around that time when David Sedaris called to tell me he had given my name to the editor of the *New York Times Sunday Magazine* because he thought I would be the perfect person to write a piece for the back page about what it's like to be beautiful. I think I thanked him. I know I wrote down the name and number he gave me.

Then I spent days feeling anxious. *How could I write that?* I thought. Would they make me submit a photo with the essay? I thought there would be people sitting around talking about how insane it was that I would be picked to write such a thing.

The girl in the video was definitely worried about how she looked. That was easier than worrying about the things that were really wrong. I could talk about folding sweaters perfectly all day long and not understand why no one was listening.

I never called the editor.

December 2013

One of my stories goes live on a literary app called *Connu*, which is advertised as work that is curated by famous writers. The founders of *Connu* went to a Sedaris show, waited in the very long book-signing line, and asked David to give them the name of an undiscovered writer whose work he admired. The editors at *Connu* market me as "a cross between Denis Johnson and Diablo Cody."

When David first told me about this and sent me their contact information, it made me feel weepy with gratitude.

May 2012

I meet the six homeschooled teenage girls who make up my private writing workshop class at the Bushnell Performing Arts Center in Hartford. David has left seven tickets for us at the box office.

"I'm here to see David Sedaris," I say to the person behind the plexiglass window. "He's expecting me."

David takes us to the green room behind the stage and invites the girls to sit down.

He knows that these girls are incredible. I've been talking about them for months. They are smart and well read and they take this meeting seriously. One poet asks him for writing advice. He is kind and funny.

"Did Cindy tell you she had a pierced nose when I first knew her, when she was nineteen years old?" he asks. "And you have to understand—no one had piercings back then. It wasn't like it is now."

I'm stunned. It's true. I had a small stud in my nose. I did it myself one night with an art school friend, both of us drunk. I don't think I've thought about it for decades.

He could have told them so many things, much worse than this and much more telling of who I was then. He picks the one true thing that actually makes me look cooler to my students, gives me some street cred, the thing that doesn't give away what a mess I was. I am moved and amazed by how socially graceful he is, how emotionally literate. It is a near-perfect encounter and he does it so casually, as if he put no thought into it.

A man comes to the door of the green room and tells David it's five minutes to showtime.

"Let's move the time up a bit?" David says. "I have some important friends here with me right now."

The girls smile the way he knew they would.

April 2010

I meet David at his hotel. We sit on a flowery chintz couch in the lobby. I tell David that my husband and baby and I live only fifteen minutes away and he tells me how much his shoes cost.

I know I'll be divorcing my husband but I'm not sure when. The ribboned box of raw cacao nib cashew truffles and ginseng almond chia brittle is the second box I've had to purchase for David. The first box was consumed by the husband.

"How was I supposed to know that was for your friend?" he asked the night before.

"Do we often have ribboned gift boxes full of expensive unknowable delicacies just sitting around in our refrigerator?" I said.

And then I went out to buy a new box from the health food restaurant.

This wasn't the first time something like this had happened. Six months earlier for the visit I had with David, I had baked two small loaves of banana bread, with the plan to bring one to David. I pulled them from the oven and slipped a knife into one loaf to see if it was cooked.

"The one I cut into is for you and the baby," I told my then-husband. "The untouched one is for David."

When I came back downstairs, my husband had eaten a slice of the untouched loaf.

"What difference does it make?" he had asked.

I want to tell David I'd accidentally married a narcissist and would be leaving him soon. I want to tell him that I'm scared that I can't earn enough of a living to support myself and my child. Scared my past could cause me to lose custody of my baby. I can't tell him these things. Instead, I show him a photo of Atlas, still a toddler, a baby.

"Is he going to grow into those eyes?" David asks.

April 2005

I walk into a Borders bookstore in downtown Boston and find the nearest employee.

"I'm here to see David Sedaris," I say.

She immediately leads me past an area where he will read and takes me down a back hallway into a private room where he sits at a table covered with stacks of books. His book *Dress Your Family in Corduroy and Denim* has just come out and David is signing stacks of copies for people who pre-ordered.

He asks me if I'm writing and I say I'm working on a couple of stories.

"Send them to me," he says.

I have a stack of David letters critiquing my stories from over the years and I know my pile will get taller. I tell him that I'm planning on returning to Haiti to paint another mural in an orphanage with the kids, volunteer work I've recently taken on.

"Maybe it seems easier to paint murals in Haiti than it would be to write," he says.

May 2004

I get a letter from London. David writes:

> *My new book is coming out, and before the tour I'm having to do a lot of advance publicity, part of which involved filling out a questionnaire for the Barnes & Noble web site. I may have the exact wording wrong, but one of the questions was 'What writer do you feel deserves greater recognition, and why?' I wrote that you most deserve it, and then I tried to describe your writing, which is where I probably embarrassed myself. I've never been very good at describing what I like, and always come off sounding like a stoned teenager. Anyway, my response was sincere.*

I read this with a few years of clean time under my belt and after I finish the letter and fold it back into the envelope, I have a craving for heroin that brings me to my knees. It blindsides me. Will good news always partner with an urge to self-destruct? I wonder. As if addiction's weight and pull feels called to show up just to say, *Remember me? I am still here waiting for you.*

August 1999

"How many times do you want to do this?" Dr. P asks me. "Aren't you tired?"

He is the tough-love psychiatrist at the Institute of Living in Hartford, where I have come for inpatient treatment after my last relapse in Chicago. I am convinced he hates me. The feeling is mutual. I hate the way he carefully mismatches his socks every day and then sits in group with one ankle displayed prominently on his knee so we can all note the eccentric purple polka dots on his left foot and the yellow stripes on his right. I hate the way he smokes in the gazebo out on the grounds where we can all see him from the window of the day room and how he uses his "smoking addiction" to highlight some of his substance abuse lessons. Each time he brings it up, I think about how my father died of lung cancer three weeks after he was diagnosed, and still I long to smoke all day every day and not just on the smoke breaks they allow us between therapy groups.

As Dr. P drones on about medication changes, I spot his tote bag leaning against the desk. The cotton straps have flopped down, leaving the contents exposed, and I can just make out the top half of the cover of *Naked*, David's newest book. I think about asking Dr. P if he likes the book. I wonder if he would think I was lying if I said I knew David. He treats all of us like we are lying every minute. For this, I don't blame him.

May 1997

David invites me to have dinner in Chicago with a small group of people, including Ira Glass.

I know that Ira has a radio show that is getting a lot of attention. Dressed up in a pin-striped suit, I sit near David at dinner. Nervous, I drink to get through dinner and I don't say much. After a recent move back to Chicago, I'm waitressing in a fancy place in the Gold

Coast where I have to memorize the ingredients in French dishes and learn the lengthy wine list.

David invites me to the next place where he and Ira and everyone else are going after dinner, a reading or literary event or something.

I make up an excuse. I want to go. I think I should go. I hate myself for not being able to go.

I drive to the West Side neighborhood where I buy drugs. By the time I am circling the blocks and looking for someone I recognize selling at the curb, I am already buzzing. There is a high before you actually use.

I feel out of place in my suit, pulling over to trade cash for tiny packages. I check my rearview mirror for police lights and I shove my purchase into my bra and put the car in drive.

Back in my tiny studio apartment, I get high. I stay up half the night rewriting the same paragraph about the people I don't know who sell to me on the corners and I imagine being a writer and going out to dinner and to interesting literary events with famous people someday.

April 1996

I meet David in the lobby at the hotel where President Reagan was shot, the Hilton on Connecticut Avenue in Washington, D.C.

I am living in D.C. after my father's death because I'm afraid to go back to Chicago right away. I'd moved back to Connecticut from San Francisco with plans to help care for my dad through his illness, but he died just three weeks after his diagnosis. Somehow, D.C. becomes a year of relief where I manage not to use drugs, although I am drinking to ease the discomfort of being me.

I meet David and his sister Amy at the Hilton after they have just finished appearing with Ira Glass to promote *This American Life*. We walk across the street to a casual restaurant and sit in a booth. David and Amy sit across from me, side by side, and they both order hot dogs.

I had met Amy Sedaris once before at a reading David gave before he published his first book or read anything on the radio. He read a story at Lower Links in Chicago. He introduced me to Amy and she leaned forward, took my hands, and said, "I've heard so much about you!" Just as I started to grin and say, "Really?" she dropped my hands and said, "Just kidding. He never said a word about you. I have no idea who you are."

I am afraid of Amy and can barely talk until she orders the hot dog and starts an easy conversation with her brother. I laugh a lot. Amy is nice and they are sweet together. David says that he is trying to finish his second book and he needs someone to hold a gun to his head.

The next day, I go downtown to a bookstore where David is reading. I meet his partner Hugh for the first time and I sit next to him during the reading. On the sidewalk after the reading, I chat with David.

I am wearing a new trench coat and oxford shoes I love. I feel far away from addiction. Clean and hopeful. The streetlights cast a warm glow. People stepping around us on the sidewalk are beautiful and not inconvenienced. They smile at me like I belong there.

In the months following that meeting, I move back to Chicago, quickly pick up my heroin habit, and finally end up in rehab with everything I own in a storage place until I stop paying the monthly fee and lose it all. Sometimes I think about specific things that had been in the boxes that went to storage, things I will never get back.

Most of the only paper copies I had of my stories, books I loved, paintings that friends from art school had made me, and the coat and shoes I loved so much.

September 1994

In San Francisco, I stop at a bookstore near the restaurant where I work. I am looking for *Barrel Fever*, David's first book.

I'm a complete wreck. I drove myself to San Francisco from Chicago after packing up everything I owned and fitting it into a rented Budget van. I left Chicago to get clean. A geographical cure is what they call it in AA. I started to go through withdrawal in Reno, Nevada. I covered the last miles shaking and throwing up into a plastic Walgreens bag. I'd bought what I thought was just enough heroin to get me across the country but I ran out somewhere around Salt Lake City.

When *Barrel Fever* comes out, I am technically clean but only because there is no powdered heroin in San Francisco and I have not yet graduated to needles. I drink and take anything I can get my hands on. It is not a good life.

When I see the cover of *Barrel Fever* with a double image of a man sticking his tongue out and David's name printed at the bottom, I immediately look for the author photo, wanting to see his face again. It feels like a lifetime ago that I last saw him.

January 1993

In a performance class at the School of the Art Institute of Chicago, I hate the way the professor starts with improv exercises, movement warm-ups. I am never good at these things, never good at being spontaneous. I watch everyone for clues and marvel at how natural they seem. Why am I the only one who feels mortified?

I am high and I feel light as the teacher shouts out, "Random walking, random walking, random walking." We are all moving through the space, weaving in and out of each other's paths.

"You and you and you," he yells out, pointing to me and two other students. "React to each other silently—I just want to see body language."

I freeze. I stay where I am. A fellow student gets on his knees on the hard wooden floor and begins to come toward me, one knee at a time. I pretend he is the boyfriend I started using heroin with. I try to make a story in my head. He is coming to save me from myself. But I am about to overdose. I jerk one shoulder. I let my limbs begin to spasm.

"Keep going," the professor says. "Interesting. Keep going."

I fall on the floor. I close my eyes and let the room disappear. I flop like a fish out of water. I listen to the teacher telling me to keep going and I have a pretend seizure. I am dying on the floor of the performance space at my ridiculously expensive art school and no one knows me at all.

"Keep going," he says again.

November 1991

The depression I've suffered from for years shifts and evolves into something I can no longer manage. I have a metallic taste in my mouth all day, every day. I completely stop sleeping but I cannot leave my bed. I suddenly find that I can't read. It's like trying to understand something in a foreign language. I might be able to grab on to a word here or there but an entire paragraph is indecipherable. I try to drink it away, which has worked in the past, and find that I somehow can no longer reach an intoxicated state. No matter how much I drink, nothing will change. There is no pleasant warmth softening the harsh sounds and lights around me, no lightness in my limbs, no humor to be found in anything. Finally, I leave Chicago to go back to my home state of Connecticut and my parents, who check me into the Yale Psychiatric Institute for most of that winter.

Months later, I get back to Chicago and sign up for classes, a performance class, and a sculpture class. I still can't read books the way I once could and I'm afraid to try to write anything. The day I register for classes, I run into Jim McManus, the writing teacher I had before David and the chair of the department. I blurt out my recent release from a lengthy stay in a psychiatric hospital.

"You're so lucky," he says. "For a writer, that's like going to war."

May 1989

David and I sit in an empty classroom to have our final meeting for the independent study I am taking with him.

"You could go to any grad school you wanted," he says to me. "You can go to Iowa if you want to. Your work is that good. You'd get in."

At the time, neither of us had any way of knowing that I would need to hold on to that moment for decades, seeing it in my mind, picturing my teacher leaning forward in his seat, hearing the exact way he said it. We couldn't know that I would close my eyes and replay it in hospitals and halfway houses for years, that it would become all I had left.

We could not have known that it would be enough. No matter how sick I was, I knew that if I showed up to a reading, David would see me. He would ask me if I was writing and he would treat me like someone who had something to say.

You could go to any grad school you wanted, I imagined him saying while I was sweating through withdrawal in scratchy hospital sheets. *You'd get in.*

September 1988

I take my second writing workshop with David and I am prepared. In the first workshop I took with him, he cut fall leaves out of construction paper, wrote our names on them, and gave us all straight pins to attach them to our shirts like third-graders. So for this second semester, I bring him a shiny red apple to secure my place as his favorite. There is a boy there rolling his eyes at the paper leaves, unable to get his straight pin through his leather jacket. Two girls make eye contact and smirk at the name tags.

This is before *Barrel Fever*, before *This American Life*, before "Santaland Diaries." This is a classroom for a required academic credit at an art school. Not just any art school, but one of the best in the country, a school where people are creative geniuses and used to being the most eccentric and talented people in whatever community they came from. I came from a small art high school in New Haven, Connecticut, and I am in Chicago now because my painting teacher said this school was the best and I got in.

But I am drowning. Every piece of art I make begins with me

trying to think of what could be good enough, unique enough. I don't ever know what I actually *want* to make anymore. I start every canvas or blank piece of paper feeling terrified. I can't make anything authentic anymore, and in every critique people sniff it out, smell my fear and manipulation immediately.

"I feel like you're trying too hard?" someone will start.

"I get what you want us to think you're saying but, like, I don't know what you're really saying in this?"

Once, in a performance art class full of talented people confessing their every true ache and embarrassment, a student no one liked gave a performance that horrified me. She was exactly what I most feared becoming in art school. She came to class on the day when she was to give her final performance and she had nothing planned, it seemed. She walked to the center of the room, a huge open space with a specially made wooden floor and a long mirrored wall. She opened a suitcase that looked like a three-year-old had packed it, a mess of clothes and toys and papers and a slice of white bread on top. She started pulling things out, and when she spoke she regurgitated pieces of other performances we'd seen just that semester from students sitting in the room making up her audience right then.

"My boyfriend said he needed space," she began. And she clasped her hands and pushed her arms out just as Bianca had done when she performed the week before.

"My grandfather used to tell me stories," she said. And she yanked her shirt off and was suddenly topless like Audrey had been earlier in the semester.

"I like to whittle," she said. And she grabbed an enormous kitchen knife from the bottom of the suitcase and held it, shifting her position and crossing her legs just as Matt had done last month for his piece.

The whole performance ended when she started to violently stab the precious floor with the knife and our teacher yelled at her and put an end mercifully to the whole thing under the guise of saving that expensive floor.

My writing classes were different. I didn't seem to have to try as hard. And although I cringed and braced myself when it was my turn to be critiqued, I would end up surprised by the reactions of other students and professors. My writing classes were the only classes where I felt I belonged in that school, that I wasn't a fraud.

David's writing workshops were unlike other writing classes at SAIC. They were unlike all other classes.

Once, to give us an example of a complicated plot, he wheeled in an AV cart with a television and VCR. He turned off the lights and we watched an episode of *One Life to Live*. I held my pen over my notebook, ready to take notes, and tried to ignore the stunned whispers around me.

There was another class where he announced that his mother would be with us the following week and our homework was to write three questions we would ask her about what it was like to raise David. She was a lovely woman in pearls and an elegant navy-blue suit. She seemed reluctant to answer our questions but completely used to the exercise of humoring her son.

January 1987

David walks into my classroom and sets his briefcase down at the head of the conference table.

Thirty years later, I can still see him standing there. I think of a story he told me long after that first class.

He was coming up from the subway on State Street, on his way to his first class as a teacher at SAIC. He was wearing a jacket and tie and carrying a briefcase, as he always did when he taught. He was not quite thirty yet and I was nineteen on that day.

David started down the sidewalk, happy, with a little swagger to his walk.

"Big Man," a homeless person yelled out to him. "You think you all that, Big Man. Look at the Big Man walking down the sidewalk."

At the time, I thought the point of the story was something like sometimes a mentally ill homeless person sees right through us and takes us down right there in the street. Sometimes that is exactly what we deserve.

Now I think the point of the story was something like we are stronger than we think, capable of surviving all kinds of abuse, as harsh as any stranger can heap on us and as dark and targeted as we can inflict on ourselves.

I think about the fact that David still came to school that day. And all the days after. And then he moved to New York and started a miraculous writing career. I think about the way his work has changed and grown. I listen to his new stories year after year in audiences of thousands of people, holding on for the next beat, the next line.

I think of David standing there in front of my class that day and I can still see him. Almost as if I understood back then that it was the day my path would swerve into new territory, where my ending would be rewritten forever.

"Hello, class," David says. "I am Mr. Sedaris."

The Tell

THEN I SHOWED HIM THE RAT PARK VIDEO,
ABOUT AN EXPERIMENT THAT SHOWED THAT
A RAT ALONE IN A CAGE WOULD SELF-ADMINISTER
DRUGS FROM A WATER BOTTLE UNTIL HE DIED,
BUT RATS IN A CAGE TOGETHER, WITH THEIR
NEEDS MET, WOULD CHOOSE PLAIN WATER OVER
THE DRUGGED VERSION. I TOLD HIM I WAS
SHOWING HIM THE VIDEO BECAUSE I ONCE USED
DRUGS TO COPE WITH MY DEPRESSION.

IT WAS COMPLETELY SILENT IN OUR HOUSE.
OUTSIDE, I COULD HEAR A CAR STARTING. I
HEARD BIRDS SINGING BEYOND OUR WINDOWS,
A DOG BARKING FROM INSIDE A NEIGHBORS HOUSE.

I PICTURED HIM AS A TEENAGER, A YOUNG
MAN, SIFTING THROUGH THIS INFORMATION
OVER THE YEARS AS HE GAINED LIFE
EXPERIENCE. PART OF PARENTING IS LETTING
THEM SEPARATE AND SEE YOU AS HUMAN
AND FLAWED. I'D HURRIED HIM ALONG IN
THE PROCESS. I WATCHED HIM TAKE IT IN.
THE ANGLE OF THE BRIGHT RAY OF SUN SHIFTED
ACROSS THE DINING ROOM TABLE.

Heartworks

IN 2009, WHEN ATLAS WAS TWO YEARS OLD AND I'D BEEN CLEAN for more than a decade, I joined a parenting co-op after seeing a handwritten sign on the bulletin board of the organic, all natural, and ethically sourced baby store where I bought all of his over-priced clothing and accessories. The co-op, named Heartworks, operated like this: for every shift, half of the parents would watch the children while the other half went to a separate quiet room to work. I thought about all the writing I'd get done and couldn't wait to get started.

Having my baby late in life, at age forty, meant that I didn't have a lot of friends experiencing early motherhood. Nearby family members offered advice that didn't feel helpful, like my Italian mother-in-law who thought I should be giving my son espresso in his sippy cup. By the time I joined the co-op, I couldn't wait to meet some like-minded parents.

Instead of renting an expensive location, one of the founders, Meredith, bravely turned her home into a day care–like space and opened Heartworks right where she lived, hosting a dozen families.

On the first day, a woman named Hibiscus introduced herself to me and said, "I gave birth in a yurt in Alaska with no electricity."

"Like, on purpose?" I asked.

I knew that unusual names for children were trendy. After all,

I'd named my son Atlas. But many of the parents at Heartworks also had creative names, as if they'd renamed themselves with one of the leftovers from their baby name list. Maybe Marigold was really Melissa or Chrysanthemum had been born Christine.

I don't want to use the real names of the kids at the co-op, so I think I can sum it up by saying that most of them were named after trees. Except for this kid Bernard, who'd been named after someone dead.

"Wow, what an unusual name!" the other parents in the co-op said when they met Bernard. This from people with children named Branch and Maple.

We fell into a routine. The day would start with Saffron, an organic raw food enthusiast, handing out smoothies that looked like the silty mud that squishes between your toes at the bottom of a dirty pond. The kids refused to drink it, except for Bernard, who would take a sip just to hold it in his mouth until he could catch a smaller child and spit it at him.

"Bernard's a total asshole," Meredith whispered to me.

In the first week, I noticed one of the mothers, Clover or Marigold or Peatmoss, following her naked one-year-old around with a portable potty. She saw me staring and said, "We're doing EC."

"EC?"

"Elimination communication. You don't have to wait until they're two or three to start potty training," she said. "EC is when you respond to babies' signals about their need to eliminate waste even before they're verbal."

I watched little Cedar pee on the floor.

One of the adults would fill the kiddie pool and everyone under the age of six would take all their clothes off and run around naked all day. Except for my kid, who wouldn't even loosen the laces of his sneakers. He liked to remain fully clothed while pushing a toy lawn mower around the yard as if he were someone's cranky suburban father.

I worried we didn't fit in. I knew that some of the parents met up on weekends and drank or smoked pot, but I made it clear right away that I wasn't available for that kind of thing. When they started the day hungover, I always felt relieved to be wide awake and hydrated, newly grateful for my sobriety. Clean, my nights were reserved for reading board books and tucking Atlas in.

There was one dad who showed up with his didgeridoo and blew into it periodically until his face was bright red. Let's call him Acorn.

"Acorn," I'd say, "I'm trying to write."

"That's so dope," he'd answer. Then he'd go back to blowing into his instrument, which was like trying to write next to an agitated baby elephant.

At snack time, Acorn would hand his daughter a carrot with the greens still attached and visible dirt on its surface, as if she were a horse. She only had two teeth.

We weren't getting much work done in the quiet room. The parents sat outside in lawn chairs, paralyzed by the heat and the boredom, while the kids took over the house. We were all so exhausted by parenting these busy tyrants.

Meredith once found her baby's bedroom covered in uncooked rice, as if a dozen newlyweds had passed through after their I-do's. Another time she found salt sprinkled all through the sheets on her bed, the empty saltshaker left as evidence under her pillow.

"Do you think if someone dumped a bag of garbanzo bean flour on top of a guinea pig, it would kill it?" Hibiscus asked.

"I mean, it's gluten-free, so . . ." Meredith answered, knowing the question wasn't hypothetical.

I once walked into the house to refill my ice water and saw little Elm and Birch patting mounds of wet sand they'd tipped out of their sandbox buckets onto the kitchen table.

"That's so dope," I said, and went back outside.

On an afternoon late in the summer, one of the EC babies was roaming around without a diaper and no one was reading her communications, so she just squatted in the backyard and eliminated a huge mess.

"No!!" we screamed.

Then before we could yell for her mother, Meredith's little corgi ran over and ate it.

"No!" we screamed.

Little Aspen came out of the house with a toothbrush and went straight for the dog.

"That's *my* toothbrush!" Meredith said, as the child shoved it into the dog's mouth.

My son toddled up to me, his polo shirt buttoned all the way up to his neck, his high-tops double-knotted, and tapped my leg, "Mama, I told you, wear your shoes."

✧

When the summer came to an end, so did the co-op. It's been ten years now and Meredith is still one of my favorite people.

We may not have gotten very much work done, but Meredith had created a community. There was comfort in seeing faces that looked as overwhelmed and stunned as my own. Parenting was the first really hard thing I'd done as a sober person and it was good to know I wasn't the only one unsure of how to do it well. Together, we watched the murmuration of our collective children. We gave ourselves room to just be, to feel the heat and let perfection go, to see who these small people were that we'd brought into the world, to be okay with ourselves in a moment when we didn't have to be defined by what we were making or doing or achieving. Heartworks accidentally gave us a pause before we got back up and applied to grad school or got divorced or went back to work.

My son is twelve and an actor now. Sometimes, on a film set, I'll look up from my book to see him working with the director and I'll think of the days when all he wanted to do was push a toy around the grass, resisting any nudge I gave him toward organized activities. Maybe he was dreaming. Maybe the naked kids in the house were finding out true things about themselves in the world without their parents hovering. Maybe *everyone* was finding themselves. And in that sense, it was everything we needed in that moment.

Gifted

ATLAS SPENT THE FIRST FEW YEARS OF HIS LIFE OBSESSED WITH ceiling fans. Even in his infancy, I could wear a necklace made of rattles and pacifiers and live fuzzy kittens and he would not take his eyes off the twirling motion above him.

Mesmerized by the sight of spinning blades, he would freeze where he stood in stores, doctors' waiting rooms, or the post office, while people glared at me and tried not to trip over him.

When he was two, the age when most kids pleaded for a trip to the park or the zoo, my son begged me to take him to Home Depot. Together, we'd walk up and down the ceiling fan aisle and I'd recite the names of all the models on display.

The fan aisle also had a section with accessories. Switch cup adapters, pull chains, light kits. Sometimes I'd let Atlas choose one item, which he'd carry around for weeks.

Once in the grocery store check-out, he sat in the cart, giddily holding to his cheek a silver pull chain with an imitation pewter fob. I busied myself piling my items onto the belt, hoping the cashier wouldn't be the kind to make small talk with my kid.

"Whatcha got there?" she said.

He held it out to show her, the chain dangling over his tiny fingers. Turning sharply to me, she said, "That's not a toy. And isn't it a choking hazard?"

"Not really?" I said. "I could pull it out by the chain if it lodged in his throat. So, no."

Another time in a park, my son walked through the play area gripping a bleached oak replacement blade, patting it as if it were a baby doll.

"Whose kid is that, kissing a piece of wood?" one mother said.

While other children enjoyed videos of Dora the Explorer or Elmo, my son was entertained by some guy on YouTube who discussed ceiling fans in endless monotonous lectures.

"Notice this antique bronze incandescent Casablanca is missing the flush-mount brushed-nickel hardware of the earlier models."

When Atlas was three and a half, a friend suggested that his obsession pointed to autism. Patting my shoulder, she said, "Just google kids plus ceiling fans when you get home. Then call me—I'm here for you." As if I'd never noticed that my kid wasn't playing with dump trucks like all the other three-year-olds.

New to the job of motherhood, I wondered if I should be more worried, especially when other people seemed to think I should be. He never liked dinosaurs or Legos but devoted a year of his childhood to a species of deepwater fish called sarcastic fringeheads. He memorized books he loved but seemed to have no number sense whatsoever. And he developed a fear of balloons that made birthday parties traumatic.

Then in second grade, my son came home with a letter announcing that he was accepted into his school's gifted program. Handing me a permission form to sign, he said, "They gave us a bunch of tests. I forgot to tell you."

I'd spent years trying to wall us off from people who saw his eccentricities negatively. Gifted hadn't occurred to me. What was I not doing for my child if I'd missed this possibility?

I found a support board online called "Parents of the Gifted and High-Achieving."

That's a little heavy-handed, I thought. *What if your kid is just a genius of ceiling fans?*

On the first thread I found, someone had posted, "My daughter doesn't relate to her peers. They purposely leave her out because they're all jealous of how advanced she is. You'd be surprised by the naked envy of two-year-olds."

Another parent wrote, "I had this problem in our first day care. My four month old was saying short phrases in both English and Finnish and the other parents were so threatened."

Halloween had just passed and the board was full of parents pretend-complaining about the costumes their darlings had chosen.

"My poor kid has to explain his costume every year. This year, he was Sir Robert Walpole, the first prime minister of England, circa 1721."

"I feel you," another parent said. "My son went as Rising CO_2 levels in the bloodstream."

"You are so my tribe," another woman said. "My daughter was Dengue Fever for Halloween this year."

"Don't get me started," said the last poster in the thread. "My kid went as her own anxiety!"

Where did these parents live, I wondered, and was anyone in their real life still speaking to them?

My son got lucky. Miss Janover, the teacher for his gifted program, wasn't like any of those parents on that board. She didn't talk about IQ scores, didn't ask how many languages her students spoke, or if they were doing our taxes by nine months old. She was never worried about my son; she said he was an artist.

But then the luck ran out. The health problems Miss Janover had endured all year turned out to be cancer. Before she died, she had a goodbye party.

When we walked into her house, she spotted us through the crowd of visitors and reached out to my son from where she sat wrapped in a quilt. Without hesitation, he crossed the room and went to her. Taking her hand, he leaned down to hear her better while she whispered in his ear. Eleven-year-old boys aren't big on holding the hands of adults. But he stayed.

I stood by the door, where the cold January afternoon blew in each time someone else arrived bearing food and comfort. Miss Janover held both his hands in her own, as if coaxing a promise from him. He nodded solemnly, oblivious to the swirl of activity surrounding them. It was just what you might expect from someone who knew before he could even walk that the world is full of beauty if you pay attention to what is spinning brilliantly before your eyes.

The Salton Sea

THE TEACHER FOR YOUR GIFTED PROGRAM CALLS ONE NIGHT AT THE END OF FOURTH GRADE. YOU REFUSE TO DO THE FINAL MAPPING PROJECT FOR THE GEOGRAPHY UNIT. I SAY I THINK YOU HAVE DYSCALCULIA, A MATH LEARNING DISABILITY. ENLARGING A MAP WITH A GRID SYSTEM IS EXACTLY THE KIND OF THING THAT IS AFFECTED BY DYSCALCULIA.

YOU AREN'T THE KIND OF SMART THAT DOES MATHEMATICAL EQUATIONS LIKE PARTY TRICKS.

I SAY YOU ARE A POET, THAT YOU JUST PUBLISHED A POEM. SHE SAYS YOU NEVER TOLD HER THAT.

HERE IS A GHOST TOWN WITH MUD THE COLOR OF DRIED BLOOD, AN ABANDONED LAKE IN THE MIDDLE OF THE CALIFORNIA DESERT, WHERE 8 MILLION DEAD TILAPIA WASHED UP IN ONE STRANGE DAY.

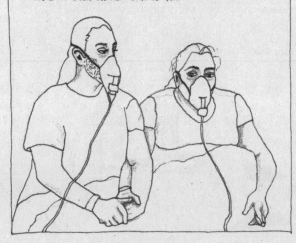

THIS IS A PLACE WITH DIRT CLOUDS THICK ENOUGH TO BLUR THE OTHER SIDE OF THE STREET AND MOST PEOPLE HAVE INHALERS AND NEBULIZERS BECAUSE THE DUST FROM THE DEAD AND DYING LAKE IS CHOKING AND CAKING THEIR LUNGS.

YOU ALREADY LIKE TO LIFT UP THE CORNERS OF LIFE AND SEE WHAT DARK THING IS GROWING UNDERNEATH. THIS IS YOUR KIND OF LANDSCAPE.

THE SALTON SEA IS YOUR POEM READY TO BE WRITTEN FROM THE FIRST IMAGE YOU SEE, THE FIRST PAGE YOU READ ABOUT HOW THIS HAPPENED AND WHY.

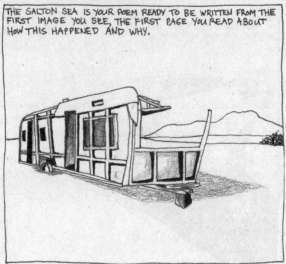

THE WORDS WILL DROP INTO PLACE,
MAPPING THEMSELVES OUT INSIDE OF YOU.

Vodka Vodka Vodka

"My fourth-grader smart-asses his way through his homework," I say. "This week, he had to write a paragraph from the prompt, 'My friend and I have so much in common,' and his first line was, 'We both still have our lives.' "

My therapist smiles, sitting across from me in her armchair. I cross my legs in my usual spot on the tweed love seat in the flesh-colored room that is her home office.

This is my first time back in therapy in over a decade. I feel rusty, like I don't know how to do this. I never want to come when the appointment arrives. I'm fine, I think. I don't feel tempted to use, I'm not depressed. I have some anxiety around my son's safety and well-being, but doesn't every mother worry?

"On the way home from school today, he said to me, 'Mom, when you use your turn signal, all I hear in my head is *vodka vodka vodka*.' "

"What I'm wondering," the therapist says, looking down at her notes, "is if maybe it's easier for you to talk about your son rather than talking about your own life."

My son is *my life*, I could say, but that's a little heavy-handed.

"Maybe," I say. "But doesn't it sound like that? *Vodka?* He has unusual word associations. He tells me whenever he says his teacher's name, Mrs. Parillo, he thinks about shrimp."

"Last week, you talked about breaking your jaw in your addiction. I wonder how hard that must have been for you," she says. "I imagine it was painful and somewhat disfiguring. Can you say more about that time?"

"It wasn't terribly painful. I kept discovering new things I couldn't do. Like blow out a candle. Or lick a stamp." I don't say that as soon as I was discharged from the hospital, I was back in the bars, sipping liquid Percocet between vodka tonics. "I lost a lot of weight, obviously, and I felt very fragile," I say. "I was dating this artist named James."

I had a few different boyfriends at the time, a collection to meet my needs. I was afraid of being sober or alone. I don't say that out loud because I don't like what it says about me.

"One night, we went to a bar in Wicker Park," I say. "These guys came in, one of them getting loud. The bartender pulls out a bat and holds it up and James gets to his feet so quickly he knocks his barstool over. A chair flies over the bar and the bartender comes scrambling over the top, knocking my drink to the floor."

My therapist holds her pen perched over the pad on her lap.

"And I had no way to get to the front door, not with all these men starting to fight. So I crawled down the length of the bar on my hands and knees, like Jackie Kennedy on the back of the limo."

The therapist laughs.

"I'm wondering if you feel like you have to entertain me," she says.

"I don't think I'm trying to entertain you," I say. "Do I seem like I am?"

"Do you feel like you are?" she says.

"What?" I say.

"Pardon?" she says.

"Oh, wait, I think I did feel disfigured at one point," I tell her. "It was the first week after I'd broken it."

"Broken . . ."

"My jaw," I say. "This restaurant owner I was seeing picked me up in his convertible to get a drink."

"Were you just out of the hospital at that point?"

"This was maybe two days after I got out," I say. "We were on Michigan Avenue and it was a sunny day. We drove down Oak Street, through the Gold Coast. All of these beautiful women were walking down the sidewalk in summer dresses and high heels, their hands full of shopping bags. I leaned against the passenger door to look in the side mirror and I looked deformed. It was the first moment I'd realized how fucked up I was. The whole side of my face was navy-blue and purple and yellow with bruising and it was huge, like a tumor."

I laugh and she looks at me.

I haven't had a drink or a drug in twenty years. I thought a therapist would beam at me, congratulate me, eyes shining with admiration. *Look at you*, I'd imagined her saying.

"And what happened then?"

"I told him to take me home."

And then I never saw him again, never answered his calls. I couldn't stand the idea that he'd seen me like that, that he knew me at my worst.

"We have to stop," the therapist says.

She walks me to the front door and closes it behind me when I step outside.

A warm spell has melted most of the snow on the sidewalk. On my way to my car, I see the house across the street, lit up and open, enormous windows like movie screens. A girl upstairs plays her flute. A man sits in the library, briefcase and laptop hinged open like clamshells. Imagine living somewhere so safe, you don't even feel the need to close your blinds to hide your luck.

In the kitchen, a boy sits at a table with his homework. He smooths and folds his paper, closes his books, places his pencil in a shiny case. A woman moves from counter to stove, busy, smiling in the golden light. She seems to say: Watch me feed my family with this whole, lemon-adorned chicken. See his homework finished and neatly put away. Look at the books in rows. My stilettos never hurt my feet. My jewelry is insured. My car is serviced regularly. My liquor bottles are expensive and dusty from neglect. They line shelves as a decoration. I only keep them for certain guests, for emergencies, for people who can't say they live here.

I am on this street because I want a therapist to help me to tell a true story about myself. I want to learn to recognize that the surface image rarely matches the history and truth underneath. I can say this out loud, but still, I stand on the sidewalk squinting at strangers, trying to convince myself.

August Afternoon

ON THE MORNING OF MY SECOND WEDDING, MY FRIEND MEREDITH CAME OVER AND TOLD ME TO LIE DOWN ON MY LIVING ROOM FLOOR BECAUSE THAT WAS THE BEST WAY FOR HER TO DO MY MAKE-UP. I FLOATED THERE WITH MY EYES CLOSED, LISTENING TO THE CHIRPING VOICES OF OUR KIDS IN THE NEXT ROOM.

I WAS MARRYING GIAN-CARL IN A TINY PARK ON MAIN ST IN MIDDLETOWN, CT, JUST A COUPLE OF BLOCKS FROM THE APARTMENT THAT ATLAS AND I HAD CALLED HOME FOR THE PAST YEAR. IT WAS A SMALL, INFORMAL WEDDING, WITH CLOSE FRIENDS AND FAMILY, ON A BEAUTIFUL AUGUST AFTERNOON.

WALKING TO THE PARK, A HANDFUL OF PEOPLE ON
THE STREET WISHED US WELL. GIAN-CARL AND I
STOPPED, MOVED BY THEIR HAPPINESS FOR US,
THOUGH WE WERE STRANGERS TO THEM.

MIDDLETOWN HAS A COMMUNITY HEALTH CENTER ON
MAIN ST, AA MEETINGS IN SEVERAL LOCATIONS, AND AN
ADDICTION TREATMENT CLINIC NOT FAR FROM DOWNTOWN.
THE PEOPLE CALLING OUT CONGRATULATIONS COULD HAVE
BEEN PEOPLE I KNEW YEARS AGO, FROM HOSPITALS,
RECOVERY HOUSES, MEETINGS. I WAS MARRYING THE
PERSON WHO KNEW THAT I WAS THINKING THERE WAS
NO REASON I SHOULD BE THE SOBER ONE IN THE
WHITE DRESS.

THE WHITE DRESS I WORE IS STILL HANGING IN MY CLOSET. WHEN I MENTION WEARING IT AGAIN SOMEDAY, MY HUSBAND SAYS HE CAN STILL REMEMBER EXACTLY THE WAY THE FABRIC FELT IN HIS HANDS. A WEDDING IS LATE AFTERNOON AUGUST SUN, GOLDENROD BLOOMING IN A CITY GARDEN, WHITE ICING AT THE CORNER OF YOUR SEVEN-YEAR-OLD'S MOUTH, YOUR NEW HUSBAND'S HAND ON THE SMALL OF YOUR BACK FOR MOST OF THE DAY.

Rated M for Mature

WHEN ATLAS WAS AN INFANT, I JOINED A GROUP OF MOTHERS who'd all had babies within a few weeks of each other. One of the moms often began sentences with, "If I were you, I would do my research." She once said this to me when I mentioned that my son liked avocados. If you questioned her, pushed for an explanation, she'd say, "Just look into it. That's all I'm saying." I don't think she had any specific information warning against avocados or pacifiers or toys made in China; she just wanted to feel like an expert, someone who could save her child from any hidden danger that might be lurking in the world.

Part of me admired her confidence. By the time my son was a toddler, the only advice I felt comfortable giving if pressed was, "Never leave a two-year-old alone in a room with someone else's newborn and a Magic Marker."

Now my son hates avocados and loves video games. He got a little obsessive when he discovered *Fortnite*, a cooperative shooter-survival game. He could play online with real kids he knew from school and I suddenly had to rethink my policy of allowing swearing. I had always pictured each curse being used separately, by itself, quietly and in the privacy of our own home.

"Hey, sweetie," I said. "I'm thinking maybe swears shouldn't be combined with specific body parts. It's maybe a little inappropriate to scream into your headset at other fourth-graders, 'I will fuck you in your eyeball if you shoot me.' "

Besides the swearing and the shooting, there were things about *Fortnite* I liked. Kids would readily admit that they were not great at this game. Even the kids who bragged about everything else seemed happy to say, "Dude, I suck." In a *Fortnite* match, sometimes enemies would stop shooting each other and instead agree to a dance-off. And there are no rigid gender roles. My son has long hair and even the boy who told him he looks like a girl seemed perfectly fine with playing *Fortnite* as a character named Dreamflower, with pink sparkly clothing, long yellow braids, and gigantic boobs. Dreamflower looks pretty even when screaming, "I will fuck you in your eyeball."

But *Fortnite* has now been replaced with *Grand Theft Auto*, or *GTA* for short. Initially I told my son he could not have this game until he turned eighteen. When his very sweet, grown-up stepbrother wanted to get it for him for Christmas, I caved. *How bad could it be?* I thought.

Grand Theft Auto comes with a "Criminal Enterprise Starter Pack." In *GTA*, when you buy an apartment with your bank heist or meth lab funds, alcohol and a bong magically appear on your kitchen counter. The name of the beer that takes up all the space in your *GTA* refrigerator is Pisswasser. The cursor for selecting things in the game is a middle finger. On the first day he played, I heard my son yell into his headset, "My P.-Diddy-ness is out of control right now!"

He asked me if I wanted to see his apartment in *Grand Theft Auto*. It was a modern, sleek high-rise that I'd like to live in myself.

"Doesn't Hadrian's avatar look like Kim Jong-un?" he said.

I leaned in closer to the screen. His friend's avatar did indeed have the exact same haircut as the leader of North Korea.

Then my son showed me the animated figure he had chosen to represent himself. A black man in a neon-pink tracksuit with a giant gold dollar sign roped over his chest, a neck tattoo, chin-length dreadlocks, and a smile covered in what my son called his solid-gold grillz.

Then he pointed out the animated figure of his other friend, Dylan. The avatar had a blond buzz cut and looked exactly like Dylan. The Dylan figure walked into a wall.

"Dylan's really drunk," my son said. "He just got back from defending his weed farm."

Characters can choose to get drunk in *GTA*. My son tells me he hates it because it makes the screen wiggly and if you try to drive one of your fancy cars, you can't get where you need to go.

"Are there twelve-step meetings in *GTA*?" I asked.

We've returned to the subject of substance abuse many times since I revealed my past. He asks me sensitive questions about those years, questions not about what I *did* but about how I *felt*.

My husband and I call my kid Aunt Ruth because he's so cautious and careful. His Instagram is full of short videos where he can be heard telling friends not to do stupid, risky things like jump from great heights or bike without helmets. He checks the expiration date on everything I feed him as if I have a rap sheet for poisoning people. When he was five, he watched some preteen boys trying to coast down an icy hill standing up on their sleds, and he put his little hands on his hips and screamed at them, "Are you crazy? Where is your mother?" Last summer, he rolled down a grassy hill on a hot day and when his body came to rest at the bottom, he stared up at the cloudless blue sky and said, "Great. I just rolled in this grass without even thinking about ticks. I'm totally getting Lyme disease now."

When I ask him if he thinks *Grand Theft Auto* could influence kids in negative ways, he says, "Maybe some kids. But Mom, I know it's just a game."

When I had my son, the world seemed to rearrange itself into an obstacle course of harm. As he grew older, the worry came down to choices about how much to shelter and protect, how much to reveal.

If another parent were to ask me if they should let their child play *Grand Theft Auto*, I would take a moment to answer. *You have to know your own child*, I might say. On other days, I might tell them, *It's pretty bad actually*. And on days when I felt completely ill-equipped to give advice, I'd say, *If I were you, I would do my research*.

Hospital Scenes

IN THE DARK MOVIE THEATER, I LEAN OVER AND WHISPER TO MY almost twelve-year-old Atlas, "This film is like a Chase Middleton photograph."

Chase was an Australian photography grad student at Yale who photographed my son inside a cinder-block building where gravestones were made and sold. The sign out front called them remembrances, but they were markers for the dead. Chase photographed my son slouched in a chair while an old man sat nearby in a flannel shirt.

"Atlas, look bored," she directed from behind her tripod.

The film is like a Chase Middleton photograph because it has the same odd color sense, a kind of matchy blandness made from a palette that feels retro in every shot. In the movie, a doctor drives around a bleached gray landscape, visiting flesh-colored state hospitals where he performs lobotomies. It's depressing in a way I hadn't counted on.

"Is this what it was like when you were in the hospital?" Atlas says.

He is asking about the first hospitalization for depression, the place where I imagine that the clock started ticking on the worst years of my life. Since I told him the story of the life I lived before he was born, his questions pop up like any other curiosity he has when he tries to picture me without him. *What was your favorite subject in third grade? Did you always know you would be a writer? Did you think you might die from depression?*

I take a handful of his popcorn and think while chewing. No one is in the theater today except for the two of us, so we can talk as much as we want. It's a quiet movie, this Chase Middleton movie.

"No," I say. "It wasn't that bleak. And we wore our street clothes, for the most part. Also, nobody performed lobotomies on patients by that time."

I don't tell him about the padded room where they put people who couldn't calm down. I never saw the inside of it because I spent my time there working hard to stay out of the isolation room, out of wrist restraints, which were just as terrible as they sound.

Then in the movie a character suddenly smashes a chair to bits in a hospital hallway under the fluorescent rectangles of light. The splintering and splitting of the wood, the way the pieces fly across the movie screen, makes me remember the time a patient named Dale smashed the unit guitar into a million pieces. The staff came running and the alarm sounded. Dale had been soft-spoken and quiet before he did that, much like the young man in the movie who breaks the chairs.

"Was anybody pacing around, all crazy like that weird guy before?" Atlas asks.

"No," I say. "Well, actually . . ."

He leans closer to me.

Actually, there was a woman named Kelsey who paced that way and who found ways to disturb the other patients who were very sick. She could bring a room full of patients nodding off on Thorazine to panicked life in seconds.

"Don't touch me, you have AIDS," she'd say to Megan, the paranoid OCD sufferer.

"You ate something that they put palm oil in," she once said to Tom, a Princeton student who'd had a psychotic break and was brought in on a stretcher screaming about palm oil contamination.

"I fucked your boyfriend when you were out on the smoke break," she said to me, the treatment-resistant depressive.

I had this boyfriend who moved to New Haven to be near the hospital for me. He worked in a warehouse and visited me at night.

"He doesn't like fat chicks," I'd said back. Kelsey was eating-disordered and I struggled to be the bigger person with people like her; I found it so easy to just sink down to their level and then find a spot even lower than that.

"Actually, *I* paced a little," I say to my son. "But not like that. I paced because I wanted to get out of that place and get on with my life and move faster toward my future because I just knew something better was waiting for me and, look, I was right, it was you."

It's strange to think about how close that hospital is to where I sit in this downtown movie theater. I have considered driving by at times, slowing near the gates that surround the small courtyard where we used to smoke. But I never have.

On the screen, the next scene is the chair-breaking character being prepped for a lobotomy.

"Mom, I'm so glad you were never in a lobotomy hospital like in this movie."

"Me, too," I say.

And it's true, I watch this movie and feel thankful that I didn't live it.

I don't tell my son that I hadn't slept for weeks before being admitted, so that when the Gulf War began during the first week of my stay and the unit television was showing green tracers lighting up the sky in real-time reporting of the war, I believed it was some kind of experiment Yale was doing on us, maybe monitoring how mentally ill people react to a war. This seems crazy now, but not as crazy as the way I sobbed for days when Gary on *Thirtysomething* died in an episode during that same hospital stay, how I wept as if he were a real person and we'd been close.

"Do you know what I remember?" I say to Atlas. "I remember this guy named Richard who was an aide, like a helper, on the unit. The aides were the people who sat with us, took us places if we had permission to leave the unit, and brought us outside for smoke breaks because we couldn't smoke inside. Anyway, one night Richard took a few of us out on the last smoke break before lights-out. We were standing outside with cigarettes and suddenly there were gunshots that sounded really close. The courtyard was walled off by a fence but it had spaces in between the slats that you could easily shoot a bullet through. When the gunshots started, Richard threw himself in front of the group of us and pushed us all down, his body sort of draped over us in protection. And I was stunned that this man whose job it was to just sort of babysit us would put his life on the line to ensure our safety. Without even thinking about it."

"Do you wish you could see him again?" Atlas asks.

"No," I say. "Not see him in person. But I wish I could send him a thank-you note, because I never forgot him. Sometimes people in this world will shock you with how good they are and you never even see it coming."

Mother Noise

I AM STANDING IN A HALLWAY IN A SCHOOL IN BROOKLYN, WAITING for Atlas to come through the metal double doors at the other end.

"Quiet on the set," the sound guy calls out. "*Born to See*, Scene Seven. And, action."

Atlas is playing a bully in this, his fourth short film. He was thrilled to land the role, but I worry about how he'll pull it off. Last month, the psychologist at his school told me that he sees Atlas holding the door for other kids and then he gets stuck there, not wanting to let it close in anyone's face, until an adult rescues him by saying, "Atlas, get to class and let them handle the door by themselves." When kids in his friend group argue, he reminds them of what they love about each other so they'll make up and be friends again. The comments on his report card are often about how kind he is.

The kid who is playing his victim leans against the wall in the hallway. Not only does Atlas have to pretend to bully a kid who is smaller than he is, but the character is also blind. And this kid is a great actor, convincingly disabled.

The doors slam open and Atlas comes through them, a crowd of kid actors behind him, playing his bully enablers, his entourage. For a second I can't believe it's my Atlas. He isn't even walking like himself. He is *swaggering*. I didn't know he could swagger.

I'm grinning like a crazy person. I cover my mouth with my hand, afraid I'll make some kind of strange, joyful, elated, weird mother noise.

Atlas goes up to the blind boy and pokes him. Toby, the actor who plays the blind boy, reaches out and tries to push Atlas back, but because he can't see, Atlas is able to hop out of his way and then shove him again, taunting him. It's a bit of choreography the two boys worked out earlier with the director in an empty classroom. It comes together beautifully as the cameraman moves in closer for the shot. The entourage laughs on cue.

Then the scene changes when the actress playing Toby's mother runs down the hallway, charging at Atlas, wanting to stop the torture of her child.

I know the scene. I helped Atlas rehearse it at home. I know what she will say. I know she puts her hands on my kid. I know she is supposed to yell at him. Any mother would act the same way in that situation.

Then she is shoving my child. He grabs her wrists when she holds his shoulders to the wall yelling, "Don't you touch him!"

My hand still over my mouth, I stare at my son's face. His expression is perfect, wide-eyed and shocked by her violence, the toughness drained away so he only looks young and vulnerable, a child, my child.

My eyes well up. Tears roll down my cheeks. I can't move. It's the emotion of the scene, the mother character's anguish, the strangeness of watching someone attack my son in front of me. But it's also seeing him be so good at this, the surprise of how talented he really is. He is all in, committed to the moment, in love with the process, the craft of this. I am witnessing someone I love discovering his passion. He has grown into this person with room to find himself, this magic piece of who he is. I don't know when this happened, only that I wanted it so badly for him.

"Cut," the director yells. "Holy shit, you guys. That was fantastic."

I watch the mother throw her arm around Atlas and hug him. They are beaming at each other, these two actors. They know they connected and found the truth of the scene, where something happens that is real.

They both look over at me. I haven't moved and I'm crying.

"Hey, Mom," the actress says to me. "It gets a little intense, I know. Are you okay?"

He's happy. He's good. He's growing up. He's thriving.

"I'm okay," I say.

I Went from Phoenix, Arizona

MY COUSIN BOBBY DIED IN EARLY 2019. HE ONCE STAYED WITH me, more than twenty years back, when he'd been sent to Walter Reed Army Medical Center after being injured during his deployment to Bosnia, and I happened to be living in Washington, D.C. We lost touch for years after that, then briefly reconnected, and then lost touch again, most likely due to my aggressive gun control posts after mass shootings.

Bobby had owned guns. I wish I could have said to Bobby that my self-righteous, political anti-gun posts were about something like wanting people to be safe. I regret not messaging him. I feel upset with myself for not reaching out, for not trying to talk to him. Because he killed himself with a gun, what I really wanted was to change gun laws so people like Bobby, good people just trying to get by, would not be able to shoot themselves in a terrible, impulsive moment that they could never change or redo. I wish I could go back in time and take Bobby's gun away myself.

Bobby and his sister Karen were my cousins on my father's side. In the space of just a couple of years, there were three deaths. First, Karen's oldest son, Reed, had died at age twenty-one after a struggle with addiction, from an adverse reaction to an over-the-counter medication. He had gone through rehab and gotten clean, but his body hadn't physically recovered and this contributed to his death. Next, Bobby shot himself one Friday night. Finally, Karen's younger son, Rush, had killed himself during what she believed was a serious mental health crisis, a break from reality, exacerbated by his brother's death about two years earlier.

Before Bobby died, I wrote a graphic narrative piece about him but I hadn't really found an ending for it. The piece was called "Cousin" and this is what it looked like:

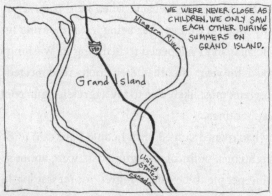

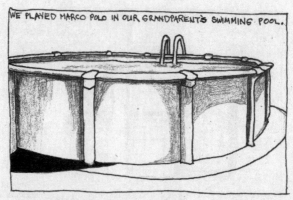

WE PLAYED MARCO POLO IN OUR GRANDPARENT'S SWIMMING POOL.

WE HELPED IN THE GARDEN.

BOBBY AND I WERE THE TWO YOUNGEST KIDS OUT OF FIVE COUSINS. HIS FAMILY LIVED IN ARIZONA, WHICH SEEMED LIKE ANOTHER COUNTRY FROM MY HOME IN CONNECTICUT. WE DIDN'T HAVE MUCH IN COMMON. HE LIKED HUNTING AND FISHING AND I LIKED DRAWING AND READING.

YEARS LATER AFTER WE'D GROWN UP AND LOST TOUCH, I WAS HOSPITALIZED SEVERAL TIMES FOR DEPRESSION AND ADDICTION.

BOBBY JOINED THE ARMY AND WAS DEPLOYED TO BOSNIA WHERE HE FELL OFF A TANK AND SHATTERED HIS ARM.

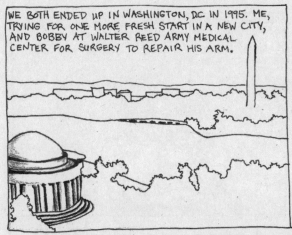

WE BOTH ENDED UP IN WASHINGTON, DC IN 1995. ME, TRYING FOR ONE MORE FRESH START IN A NEW CITY, AND BOBBY AT WALTER REED ARMY MEDICAL CENTER FOR SURGERY TO REPAIR HIS ARM.

MY DAD HAD JUST DIED OF LUNG CANCER. BOBBY WAS HIS ONLY NEPHEW. I WENT TO VISIT AND OFFERED BOBBY MY SPARE BEDROOM FOR HIS RECOVERY.

BOBBY HAD THREE DAUGHTERS AND A PREGNANT WIFE IN A NEARBY MOTEL, COURTESY OF THE U.S. ARMY.

IT WAS DECIDED, THEY ALL CAME TO STAY WITH ME AT MY APARTMENT IN CAPITOL HILL FOR THE DURATION OF BOBBY'S TREATMENT.

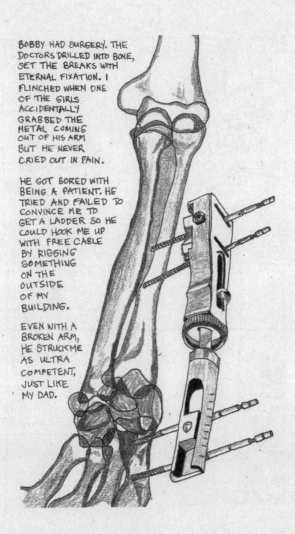

BOBBY HAD SURGERY. THE
DOCTORS DRILLED INTO BONE,
SET THE BREAKS WITH
ETERNAL FIXATION. I
FLINCHED WHEN ONE
OF THE GIRLS
ACCIDENTALLY
GRABBED THE
METAL COMING
OUT OF HIS ARM
BUT HE NEVER
CRIED OUT IN PAIN.

HE GOT BORED WITH
BEING A PATIENT. HE
TRIED AND FAILED TO
CONVINCE ME TO
GET A LADDER SO HE
COULD HOOK ME UP
WITH FREE CABLE
BY RIGGING
SOMETHING
ON THE
OUTSIDE
OF MY
BUILDING.

EVEN WITH A
BROKEN ARM,
HE STRUCK ME
AS ULTRA
COMPETENT,
JUST LIKE
MY DAD.

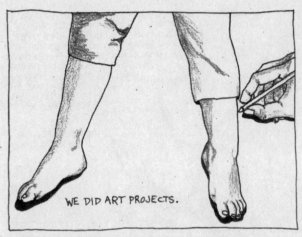

WE DID ART PROJECTS.

THERE WAS NEVER SILENCE TO THINK TOO MUCH AND I COULD
CALL THOSE SWEET GIRLS MY FAMILY.

BEING AROUND BOBBY MADE ME THINK OF MY DAD.
EVERY NOVEMBER, THE MEN IN MY DAD'S FAMILY
CAMPED OUT IN THE COLD TO HUNT DEER.
I WAS NEVER INVITED BECAUSE I WAS
FEMALE, NOT THAT I WANTED TO GO
ANYWAY. SOMETIMES, WITH BOBBY
AROUND, I FELT LIKE MY DAD
WAS STILL ALIVE AND
I COULD CALL HIM
WHENEVER I WANTED.

"GUESS WHO'S HERE?"
I IMAGINED SAYING.

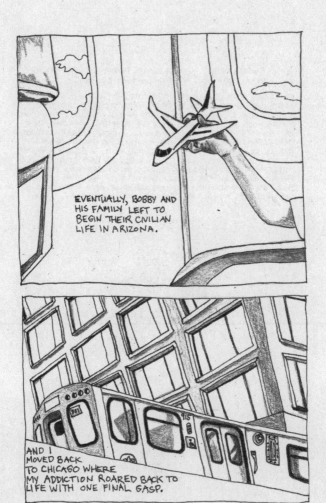

YEARS PASSED. BOBBY'S KIDS GREW UP. TWO OF HIS DAUGHTERS HAD KIDS OF THEIR OWN. AND I HAD ATLAS BY THEN.

ONE DAY, I WATCHED A VIDEO THAT ONE OF THE GIRLS HAD POSTED. BOBBY WAS BACK IN THE HOSPITAL FOR SURGERY DUE TO AN INFECTION IN HIS ARM AT THE SITE OF THE ORIGINAL INJURY. FOR SIX SECONDS, HE SAUNTERED DOWN THE HOSPITAL CORRIDOR LIKE HE WAS ON THE CATWALK. A GROWN MAN, A GRANDFATHER, DOING HIS IMPRESSION OF A RUNWAY MODEL TO MAKE HIS DAUGHTER LAUGH BEFORE HE LEFT HER FOR THE OPERATING ROOM. IN SOCKS AND PAJAMAS UNDER A DENIM SHIRT WORN LIKE A ROBE, HIS HAIR STILL MILITARY SHORT, HIGH AND TIGHT. FOUR SECONDS IN, SHE GIGGLES. IT BREAKS THE ACT, HE FACES THE CAMERA STRAIGHT ON AND GRINS AT HER. THOSE LAST TWO SECONDS SEEMED LIKE PROOF OF A HAPPY LIFE. BUT OUR LIVES ARE ALWAYS MORE COMPLICATED THAN THAT.

❧

About nine months after Bobby's death, I flew to Arizona to open for David in Tucson. I briefly met Bobby's family in Tempe for breakfast and my cousin Karen, Bobby's sister, whom I hadn't seen since childhood, drove down to Tucson with me for the show. Karen's youngest son had died only a couple of weeks before I got there.

I saw Karen walking toward me on a Phoenix sidewalk that November on a brilliantly sunny day. I was holding the heaviness of her loss in my chest, nervous about what I could possibly say to her. I had always looked up to Karen when I was a child; she was so beautiful and smart. When I saw her coming toward me in Phoenix, I wasn't sure it was her, but also, I knew it was her. I just still knew her. Even from half a block away, she seemed like someone in shock, someone numb and moving in a dream.

If you love someone when you are eight years old, it doesn't matter how many years go by without seeing them, you will still love them later, too.

❧

Three months later, Atlas and I landed in Phoenix, picked up our rental car, stopped for tacos, and drove to our Airbnb, where we chose which bedroom we each wanted. He loved Phoenix immediately because he thought it was what Los Angeles might look like, since he dreams about living there someday when he's a grown-up actor/filmmaker.

In Arizona, I couldn't stop eating. Something had slipped away from me, the structure I imposed on myself, the routine that held me together in my regular life. I am a person who struggles with moderation. I'm sober now, so it's never drugs or alcohol that I use to try to regulate my emotional state. Mostly it's food. Or procrastination, like I can't get to work until I read hundreds of pages of something or refold everything in my drawers or research something I don't need to know anything about, like wigs. Or shop online for clothing I'm not going to buy, spending hours picking just the right thing, only to end up deleting it from my cart.

In Arizona, I had a song that I hated stuck in my head almost constantly if no one was talking to me.

I went from Phoenix, Arizona
All the way to Tacoma, Philadelphia, Atlanta, L.A.

In Arizona, my plan had been to eat sensibly and make good choices. I knew I had to be on a stage in front of a couple of thousand people in a few weeks and I had clothes hanging in my closet that I needed to be able to fit in.

But I kept eating. It was as if someone had loosened the laces holding me together. Something shifted enough to disorient me into this obsession. The mix of childhood memories, the idea of overwhelming grief all around me, my own history following me like a cloud waiting to be asked about by well-meaning family making conversation, all of it filling up space inside of me that suddenly needed to be filled with anything else. At night, after Atlas had fallen asleep, I perused restaurant menus online, looking for all the things in Phoenix I'd like to eat, with one hand in the box of Cheez-Its I had purchased for Atlas. I don't even like Cheez-Its.

🖝

The next day, we drove to Tempe to see my cousin Bobby's wife, Kim, and his kids and grandkids, in the house where they all lived. The house where Bobby killed himself a year earlier. It was a nice neighborhood, with neat one-story homes, gravel gardens with cacti.

I sat with Kim at her dining room table. The one-year anniversary of Bobby's death had just passed. Next to me, there was a glass cabinet with photos and treasures celebrating Bobby. A decorative box with his ashes sat on top of a side table. Bobby's three daughters, all in their twenties, lived in the house with their mom. Two of the girls had two children each, so there were four adorable kids running in and out of the room. They wanted to color with Atlas. They wanted to play house with Atlas and they wanted him to be the dad.

"Sure," he said. "I'd love to be the dad."

He was still a kid to them, although he was twelve and they were seven, five, four, and two. Because he's an only child, this was a novel experience for him, having so many little faces looking up at him, pulling on him, hugging him.

I told Kim I wanted to write about Bobby and asked if that would be okay. I promised to show her what I wrote before I published anything. She very kindly said yes. And then she started to tell me about that night.

"I had ordered some subs that night," Kim said. "I said,

'Bob, what do you want to eat?' and that's what sounded good to him."

Out of nowhere, I had the clearest memory of a night twenty-five years earlier when Bobby and Kim were staying with me in D.C. and she said she felt like having lime sherbet, a pregnancy craving, and he walked to the corner store down the block with his fucked-up arm and its metal and bandages and got her the sherbet.

"And he had only been drinking on Friday nights then," she said. "He'd just gotten the diabetes diagnosis when he'd gone in for the surgery on his arm, so he cut down on his drinking by a lot."

I could hear the little kid voices down the hall with Atlas. Harleigh, the youngest at almost two years old, came in and out of the room to say hi and bye to me again and again.

Kim told me that Bobby's surgery was not a success. This was a surgery to address an infection from the site of the original surgery twenty-five years earlier in D.C., from falling off the tank in Bosnia. Bobby had lost all the feeling in his thumb, she said, and they wanted to go back in since they guessed they had accidentally nicked a nerve. And Bobby was very unhappy about this and was struggling a lot with the diabetes diagnosis. He had just gone off insulin right before this, she said, on his own, out of frustration.

It made me think of the last three weeks of my father's life, when he was on oxygen at home and dying of lung cancer. One day he got so frustrated with being sick and limited in what he could do that he just pulled the oxygen tube from his nose, got up, and said he was going out. He started up the stairs and was so winded by the time he reached the top, he just sat down until he could get back in bed.

"And that night, he went out to the garage and was getting worked up and I told him to come sit down and eat. But then he started yelling. And little Daniel was at the table and started crying. Natty was in the bath, so I told Chelsea to get her out and get the kids out of the house."

This was a hard story. Kim's face crumpled in tears as she told it. And then I worried that maybe she thought I wanted her to tell it because I had said I wanted to write about Bobby. I was horrified for a moment, thinking I was opening this up. But then, she seemed to need to tell it.

Bobby took a drink of whiskey in the garage. He came back in and yelled, mostly about no one listening to him. Kim tried to talk him off the ledge and get him to sit down to eat. She thought maybe he needed insulin, that he was having low sugar or something, that it was a medical crisis.

And then he went for the guns.

Kim begged him not to.

Then the girls, Kim, and the grandbabies ran outside and across the street to call 911. And then they heard the shot.

Kim ran back into the house and started CPR. She had nursing skills.

At the table, in her dining room, as she told me this, she sobbed. She said he was still alive. And she kept working to keep him breathing.

Soon the paramedics and a SWAT team arrived and pulled her away. She cried, telling me that she felt like if she had been allowed to keep performing CPR and to stay with him, he might have survived.

Chelsea, Bobby's oldest girl, came back from Walmart and gave me a framed photo of her dad. In the picture, he poses like a supermodel, sitting in a dad recliner, glasses and mustache, one hand behind his head, eyes wide, coy smile on his lips. I keep the photo on a shelf in my office now.

My cousin Bobby's youngest child, his namesake and the only boy, called Bubba by his mom and sisters, arrived toward the end of our visit from the base where he lives as a Marine. When I met him in November, he had given me dog tags with his name on it for Atlas. Because Atlas is obsessed with changing his last name to House, he wears the Robert House dog-tag necklace almost every day.

When Bubba walked in, the room came alive. His sisters and mom hugged him and his baby niece ran right for him with her arms out. Harleigh practically launched herself into her uncle's arms.

🖎

The next day, Atlas and I drove north to see Bobby's sister, Karen, where she lived in Prescott. It was about a two-hour drive into the mountains.

We found Karen's street and then we found the mobile home park and number six, where she lived. She had called it her 1970s trailer. It was raining hard when we pulled up. I parked under a little carport, behind her Subaru. She came out the side door and I hugged her and introduced Atlas.

We went inside the trailer and sat down. It smelled good and was cozy and neat.

Karen perched stiffly in an armchair, the rain outside beating against the roof. I could tell she was struggling in her grief, just trying to get through the visit. I didn't know what to do for her.

I noticed the paintings she had on her walls. One was by her son, Rush, a landscape of the beach on Lake Michigan.

"It's so bad right now," she said. She looked fragile and bewildered, like someone who had just survived a violent car crash and had stumbled in out of the rain, shocked to find herself alive and breathing.

꙼

We went to an Italian restaurant in downtown Prescott. It had mostly stopped raining but it was cold and raw outside, much colder than Phoenix.

Bobby's daughter Kendall had told me about an experience Karen had had speaking to a medium and I asked about it.

"Bobby was coming through really strong at first, desperate to talk and happy I was there," Karen said. "He didn't mean to do it."

There had been no note. Every detail I'd heard about that night said it was impulsive.

I understood how that could happen. I understood completely how you could be dead when you didn't mean to kill yourself.

More than once, I'd swallowed a bunch of psychotropic drugs I'd had around and still woken up, surprised and miserable. Once I'd sat in a car that was running inside a closed garage, reclining the seat and waiting to fall asleep. But I couldn't sleep, got bored, and didn't know how long it would take, so I turned the car off and went inside the house to bed. These instances had been years and years ago and it was hard for me to even remember feeling like that. It's hard to comprehend that I was the same person, still me, just not wanting to be alive.

"The medium mentioned PTSD," Karen said. "She told me that she wouldn't even say what she was seeing, things Bob had seen in Bosnia, too disturbing for her to even describe to me."

In Washington, D.C., Bobby had talked about Bosnia. Mostly he told me that I couldn't imagine it, that it was a nightmare with buildings that had been bombed, people just gone.

"She knew about his arm and then she said something about his eye burning, and Bobby had an eye injury at work recently that bothered him," Karen said. "How could she possibly know that?"

I told Karen I didn't disbelieve. I said I was open to the idea of what she experienced. I wasn't skeptical. The truth is, I know I might look for the same kind of thing if I had to mourn someone I loved.

"The boys were together, lots of playful energy coming through, she said. Rush feels like it was a stupid thing to do, she said. A mistake."

I looked at Atlas and he was every bit as absorbed as I was. Karen's green-blue eyes were welling up. The restaurant was drafty and I felt brittle, disoriented, achingly sad for my cousin. How were we sitting there, talking about the missing? I didn't feel like any of it was real.

I asked her if it was comforting to talk to the medium.

"I think so," Karen said. "It makes as much sense as anything else right now."

We talked about our grandfather and how he liked to polish stones and make jewelry. The last time I saw her in November, she told me two amazing stories about Grandpa House.

The first was that once he read a letter from me in front of Karen and he said, "Your cousin Cindy is a really good letter writer for a little girl. Bet she grows up to be a writer." *This is a little piece of something I will hold on to for the rest of my life*, I thought after she said it.

Then she told me about a time when she was young and her mother had just started a huge, chaotic fight with everyone while they were all at Grandma and Grandpa's. And this happened a lot. She stormed out of the house, and when it was quiet our grandfather said to Karen, "I hope you know that none of this is your fault in any way, and it never was." Karen said she held on to that for all of her childhood, because no one had ever said that before and she needed to hear it. How did he know to say that to a small child suffering like that? Our grandfather worked in a coal mine and then a factory and he was good at fishing and hunting deer, but he'd never been to therapy and men from his time didn't read about child development or feelings or anything like that. So how did he know the best thing to say to Karen? His instinct was to prevent the damage if he could.

↜

We left Prescott in the late afternoon, just as the sun started to come out. On the way up the rain and the fog had hidden a lot of the view, but now I could see how strange and vast the terrain looked, mountains layered upon mountains, rocky red sand dotted with giant cacti as far as I could see, shadows from the lingering clouds blanketing the earth below in patches.

The feeling of driving a rented car in an unfamiliar landscape flooded me with memories of the time I drove the rental van from Chicago to San Francisco. Every gas station and rest stop was filled with strangers and I was sure I would never be known again.

I looked in the rearview to catch a glimpse of my son, to remind myself that this was not then. He had his AirPods in but he smiled at me when he saw me staring and then pulled them out and said, "Yes?"

"Nothing," I said. "I just need to stop for gas."

❧

I didn't know my cousin Bobby well, but when he stayed with me, it strikes me now and has been something I've thought about over the years, that it was unbelievably stress-free, that visit. I think that was because the whole family was happy and delightful to be around. Back then, I'd hoped that if I ever got married, I would be as happy as Kim and Bobby seemed to be. The girls waited patiently for me to wake up in the mornings, whispering to let me sleep in because I worked nights. They said please and thank you and I can't recall a single tantrum. Bobby picked them up, cut their food, kissed their injuries, just as much as Kim did. It is hard to imagine me doing this now, moving a cousin and his wife into my home, people I really didn't know, along with their nine-month-old, three-year-old, and four-year-old, and have everyone be so peaceful and relaxed and happy with the arrangement.

Whatever had gone on over the years for my cousin to bring him to the night he killed himself was not a story about an inherently fucked-up person or a dysfunctional family or, really, personal failure in a way that can make other people feel better, like it couldn't happen to them. What happened to Bobby, I have come to realize, what happened to my father's side of the family, was about the ways that life can wear us down in America. I don't know every detail of his life, but it just seems to me that things should have gone better for that young soldier and his family. He was filled with good intentions and had many of the same qualities that had made my father a good man: dependable, great work ethic, devotion to his family. He should have been able to easily buy a home. He should have had much better medical care for the rest of his life. His kids should have had access to college without having to take on massive amounts of debt. Maybe any one of these issues being addressed would have kept my cousin Bobby alive. And better mental health treatment alone might have saved his nephews.

I think about me and my cousins playing Marco Polo in my grandparents' pool when we were children. I picture Bobby and me, treading water in the summertime, a soldier and an addict born from those small bodies staying afloat. It's hard to imagine what was waiting for us then that we couldn't see, our futures a dream, a mist, a fog. And the next generation after us, Karen's sons and Bobby's kids and their kids and my Atlas. And all this time, a thread connecting all of us but who knows why we got what we got, did what we did, lived what we lived? The predispositions to tragedy that lived in our ancestors radiating out like rays of the sun, stretching and reaching into the future. We can only try to prevent the same misery from visiting those who come after us, knowing as we do about the pageant of horror that could happen, that did happen, that we can't stop from happening. What other choice do we have?

❧

About a year after Bobby and Kim had left D.C. and moved to Arizona, one desperate night in Chicago, I called Bobby and asked if he would wire me money. I am mortified to think of it now. He had just started working a civilian job and they had four kids to support. I don't know if he knew about the shape I was in exactly, but he was so kind on the other end of the phone. So nice. He really wanted to help me, he kept saying, but he just didn't have it then.

All these years later, I still regret putting him in that position and it is still one of the worst moments in my addiction, one of the memories that rushes shame into my chest and makes it hard for me to breathe.

❧

If I wrote an ending to my graphic narrative piece, I'd draw a picture of Reed and Rush, an image of the two of them like vapor in the air around us, desperate to tell the medium the things they didn't get to say. Maybe I'd float Bobby with my dad and my grandfather above them, content to watch and wait for their turn to speak to the living, the rest of us left behind, startled to find ourselves upright and forced to keep going, our ears always cocked and listening for one last word, one more moment to understand each other.

Urgent Care

ON THE DAY THAT OUR CITY ANNOUNCED THE CLOSING OF schools due to the pandemic, Atlas injured his ankle in our neighborhood park. When I went to pick him up, he hopped toward my car with his arms thrown around the shoulders of two close friends. His face looked pale. It wasn't like him to make such a fuss, having me drive those few blocks to get him, needing friends to half carry him to my car. I knew he'd broken a bone.

We came home so I could figure out where to take him for treatment and so I could get his shoe off to have a look. I gave him some Tylenol and loosened the laces of his high-top, then gently wiggled his foot free. His skin was already bruising beneath the ankle bone and the swelling extended to his heel and over the top of the foot.

I contacted a mom in the neighborhood, Jen, who worked at Yale New Haven Hospital to ask if she thought I should bring him downtown to her ER.

"No way," she said. "Take him to Branford Ortho Urgent Care—they'll X-ray him on site and no one will be sick in the waiting room with corona."

It is hard to be a mother in an emergency. I'd only had one other time when Atlas needed me in that way. It was an asthma attack when he was four. It began with a chest cold. At first I was calmly taking care of him through the illness, giving him fluids, checking his temperature, reading to him in bed. And then he took a turn for the worse, and by the time I reached his pediatrician's office, I found myself running down a sidewalk with Atlas in my arms, screaming at people to get out of my way. His doctor treated him on the floor of her waiting room that day and then walked us over to urgent care, where they told me they might have to call an ambulance to take him to the children's hospital. They didn't. We went home with prescriptions and a nebulizer in the shape of a puppy.

Kids love to talk about the moments when their parents were scared, the harrowing near-misses of childhood, the incidents that were *serious*. Atlas remembers his chest X-ray and the mask I held over his mouth and nose because he wouldn't let the nurse do it. I remember the way his chest caved in so deeply with each breath on the floor of the waiting room, the peculiar gray-blue tint to his lips, my racing fear.

As I helped him hop through the front door of Branford Ortho, he felt so heavy. It was strange to have this big kid hanging off of me, needing me just to get into the building.

By then it was almost dark out. The place was empty, so they saw him immediately. He had fractured the growth plate at the end of his tibia. He was given a boot and crutches and instructions to ice and elevate, and we were on our way home.

✦

In 2017, on my fiftieth birthday, I sat in the waiting room of the ER at Yale New Haven Hospital. It was just past midnight, so I'd been fifty for about twenty minutes.

The waiting room was almost empty, just one couple on the

other side, the people sitting at the reception desk, and a couple of security guards. I had hoped my friend Jen might be working the desk but I guessed it was her night off. Her twin girls were friends with Atlas and she always made me laugh.

The right side of my face was killing me. I had pain all along my jawline and I could feel a lump beneath the skin. I originally broke my jaw in my mid-twenties, and right around age thirty I needed bone-graft surgery because it hadn't quite healed right. I assumed I had another problem after all these years.

I'm not a person who sees doctors very often. It has to be bad. In the days leading up to my fiftieth birthday, the pain got worse and worse. My MFA thesis was due in a matter of days and I had a graduating seminar to get ready to teach and I couldn't think straight from the pain. For years, one of my biggest fears, something I tried not to even think about, was that something excruciating would happen to me physically and I'd be left to suffer through it because I worried that even one painkiller could send me back twenty years to who I used to be. And that night, just before midnight, I got into my car because my biggest fear had arrived.

Once I finally got taken back to the actual ER, it was packed. The waiting room was empty, I guess, because all of their patients that night had come by ambulance. The lights were brighter, the staff rushed around hectically, the patients were loud.

I sat on a gurney with my book in my lap and watched.

Across from me, a young girl lay on a stretcher in the fetal position, asleep, her ponytail hanging off the edge. I leaned forward to peer over the foot of my bed to see if her hair was touching the floor. It wasn't. She was sleeping because she had drunk herself into unconsciousness at a party in her dorm. I heard a doctor telling her roommate that she had probably saved the girl's life by calling an ambulance.

There was a man handcuffed to his gurney near the center desk, a police officer standing next to him to tell him to watch his mouth every time he called a nurse a name. Intoxicated by something I couldn't identify from his behavior.

The hospital that night on my birthday reminded me of other hospitals, of being alone in a brightly lit bay of suffering, where I envied the people in blue, those professionals rushing around, with all of their self-esteem. People with makeup and fitness regimens and special shoes to support their arches, saying things to the patients like, "Sit tight," while they called insurance companies for permission to admit. I thought of socks with grippy bottoms and thin bleached sheets, the loose ties of hospital gowns. I thought of times I sat with alcoholics and addicts, waiting for Librium or methadone, something to take the edge off, like starving children with our hands out for a crust of bread.

But that night, it was just this lump along my jaw, pain there on that side of my face. I waited like a normal person, like a mother, like someone who'd had a shower that morning and accomplished things, someone who made dinner and did laundry and smelled nice.

ר

On the day Atlas broke his ankle, at about ten that night, his pain intensified. He had never had an injury that required an X-ray or stitches or a doctor visit. His suffering took us both by surprise. I gave him more Tylenol and my husband rushed out to pick up Motrin so we could alternate. He slept fitfully. I know this because

I stayed up all night on the little couch in his room, timing his doses of Tylenol and Motrin, watching him writhe and moan in his sleep.

By the next day, when Atlas wasn't eating very much and was still complaining of a lot of pain, I called first the urgent care clinic and then his regular pediatrician. When I explained that he wasn't sleeping or eating because he was in so much pain, they suggested the things I was already doing for him.

I wanted to say that he needed narcotics. A wave of leftover, decades-old shame ran through me, as if I were asking for myself. I wanted to rattle off the list of opioids and scream that any of those would work because *he needs something, do you hear me?*

The pediatrician suggested arnica, a homeopathic remedy for bodily trauma, which I knew about but had forgotten. I took a deep breath.

It was true that he was a little better than he'd been through the night. And my preference would be that opioids never enter his system for the rest of his life. I was well versed in the evil of painkillers, and he was only twelve years old.

My husband went out to pick up arnica at the Whole Foods in the next town over. I sat with my son and said that I wanted him to keep his leg elevated all day long and have him not move from the couch. We would stay on top of every dose of Tylenol and Motrin and add the arnica, too. We would ice it some more.

I reminded myself that he is stronger than I think. That the pain would improve, that I could see him through this. And then I brought him snacks all day and watched *The Office* with him and timed his doses and slept there on the couch in his bedroom for another night. I watched him sleep that second night and hoped the injury could be proof for him that he could get to the other side of something awful, a memory to be used later, to tell himself we survive these things. He knows how to survive.

ペ

The ER doctor finally got to me. She closed the curtain around my gurney and looked at my information on her clipboard. She felt along my jawline with her warm fingertips and looked in my mouth and said that she believed I needed to see a dentist for something like a root canal.

"Oh," I said. "You think that's all?"

And then I cried. I hadn't realized how anxious I was until that moment. I told her I was an addict afraid of pain, afraid of not being able to treat any pain I might have. Just saying it out loud in that ER was a relief. I had never been open with regular doctors, afraid of being treated badly, so I just avoided seeing them.

Then she did something amazing. She pulled up a chair and sat down and talked about pain management for addicts. She drew a picture for me of ways to prevent both suffering and relapse. She was a little younger than me, with springy curls and a kind face. She made eye contact. She touched my knee. She did not pity me or condescend or act surprised by my confession. She treated me like a whole person, not an addict. She washed away twenty years of avoiding doctors. I had been living like a fugitive, a person who had so much to hide.

ペ

After the second night, Atlas woke up feeling much better. I remembered that at age five he had fallen into a swimming pool fully clothed during visitation with his father and stepmother. He couldn't swim. They had dragged him to some friend's cookout and I suspect they did not watch him by the water, perhaps were completely oblivious to the idea that you must watch small children who cannot swim around pools. That day, my ex-husband brought him home early, walked him to my front door where he stood soaking wet and screaming, his tiny Pumas making a squelching sound with every step. They did not even seem to try to comfort him or change his clothes, they just handed him over, hysterical and dripping. I pulled him into my house and shut the door quietly while my ex-husband started to explain what had happened. I could barely hear him over Atlas's wailing, and anyway my kid was a more reliable narrator about what went on during visitation than his dad. I sat on the floor with my wet child and held him until he stopped crying, hyperventilating, screaming that he fell "under the water."

For years afterward, I pictured the moment he slipped into that pool, saw him floating in crystal-blue water, terror on his small face, eyes wide, with nothing to grab on to, disconnected and untethered, his tiny body reaching and sinking.

Sometimes you move yourself out of the darkest parts of your past in such incremental steps that at first you don't even realize you've crossed to the other side and now stand somewhere new. One day I noticed that whenever I remembered the pool incident, I no longer saw the boy underwater. I didn't imagine the bubbles leaving his mouth, the panic and the clawing and the shock of the plunge. Instead, I pictured him rising from the blue, buoyant and sure, his whole being pushing through the dappled skin of the water's surface, filling his lungs with the sweet air all around him.

🖛

The next morning, I found a dentist and had a root canal. And just like I confided in the ER doctor about my past, I did the same with the dentist. And it was fine.

If the opposite of addiction is connection, then a true story can save your life. It took me years to tell most people about my history and then more years to write this book.

What I didn't know at first was that connection starts with being whole. You can't connect when you are hiding, splintered, a mere fragment of who you truly are.

For years I imagined the me that lived through my past as a kind of a shadow, a separate secret version of myself that no one should see. But now when I think of who I used to be, I see a ghost that came home, a spirit that slipped back into the rest of me and settled in for good, finally stitched into the story of my life, synced up and humming along with the everyday beat and flow of my heart.

CINDY HOUSE is an essayist, a short story writer, an artist, and a regular opener for David Sedaris on his tours across the country. She studied at the School of the Art Institute of Chicago and earned an MFA from Lesley University in 2017. She lives in New Haven, Connecticut, with her son.